FINANCIAL FREEDOM

on-the-go

On-the-go Series is a summary of honest, complete, and practical wisdom on important topics for humanity.

Upcoming titles include:

Weight Loss
Leadership
Diabetes Type II
Emotional Intelligence
Insomnia
Asthma
Healthy Cooking
Communication Skills
Allergies
Spirituality
Anxiety & Depression

FINANCIAL FREEDOM

on-the-go

Honest. Complete. Practical.

ANDREW JEVON

Financial Freedom on-the-go™
Published by Wishing Bell Pty Ltd
Email: info@onthegoseries.com
Website: www.onthegoseries.com

National Library of Australia Cataloguing-in-Publication entry

Jevon, Andrew.

    Financial freedom on-the-go : honest. complete. practical

    ISBN 9780646567198 (pbk.)

    Series: On-the-go; 1.

    Finance, Personal--Australia
    Debt--Australia.
    Saving and investment--Australia.

332.02401

Printed and bound by Griffin Press, Salisbury South, South Australia

DISCLAIMER

The aim of this book is to provide general information, and to educate, in regard to the subject matter covered. Every effort has been made to ensure that the contents are accurate and current at the time of publication. However, the laws relating to taxation, social security, and the investment and handling of money are constantly changing. Neither the author nor the publisher may be held responsible for any action or claim resulting from the use of this book or any information contained in it. Information in the book is in no way intended to replace, or supersede independent or other professional advice. It is recommended that you seek independent and professional financial advice before proceeding with any action.

*To those who respect, appreciate, and embrace
the currency of love more than the currency of money.*

CONTENTS

Acknowledgments

Introduction

The Mind-set of Financial Freedom | 1

This is the most important part of the book. Having the right mind-set is a prerequisite to your financial freedom. This is where you will learn how to think in order to know how to be and therefore, how to act and achieve results in your life. You have to be continually reminded of your positive mind-set because this is where it all starts and where it should never end.

The Strategy of Financial Freedom | 43

You need a positive direction and strategies to achieve your financial freedom. Your mind-set must be deeply rooted in your character, but that alone won't be enough. You need to know every technical aspect of financial freedom. This is where you will understand the what, why, who, where, when, and most importantly, how to start the journey.

The Action of Financial Freedom | 103

This is where you will implement your mind-set and strategies in real life to achieve your financial freedom. This is where you will take concrete steps in creating opportunities for yourself. Everybody's situation is different, but you will understand how everybody can eventually arrive on the same destination.

Q&A Session | 117

This is where we will discuss some common questions in regard to financial freedom to complete your understanding.

ACKNOWLEDGMENTS

To the living Christ in the utmost high, the Creator of all things, the real and loving God, who made it possible for me to share the beautiful things He has given me abundantly and who has bestowed on me the greatest gifts of all— redemption, eternal life, and moral wisdom to use the riches He gave me at birth, consisting in the power to control and direct my own mind to whatever ends I desire on earth. I thank You every day that You have revealed Yourself not to the learned and the self-righteous but to the humble and the undeserving.

To the one woman I love and respect the most in this world, my mother, who taught me love so I can now share it with others, who showed me the right things in life so I now fear God and have courage in life, who lead by example so I can now be grateful to know that you prioritize my life over yours, who is happy for me and accepts me for who I am in all my strengths and weaknesses. Thank you for giving me something so grand that I shall never be able to fully appreciate, let alone give back.

To my brothers, who are with me both in good and bad times, through joy, laughter, and tears. Thank you for being there for me all the time. I can't imagine my life without you two, and I thank God every day for such grandiose blessings. I will treasure our memories until the end of time.

And to all my past and present families and friends. Thank you for making me who I am today. Thank you for enriching my life with your presence, your warmth, and your love.

To everyone who has made the production of this book possible. Authors alone can never be given the sole credit for any of their books. I'm very thankful to Edilson Marks, Jane Cole, Sam Daniels, Carolyn Gambito, and the team at Xlibris. A very special thanks to Sharon Flindell for giving me generous answers when I needed them the most. Dani Hardy at Griffin Press, Maria Watt at Thorpe Bowker, and every other staff involved whose name I would never know, but whose help I'm very grateful for. Thank you for helping me with my mission in life.

And finally, to you my dearest reader. You are the reason for this book to exist. Your plea, your courage, and your love motivated me. It is my deepest intention that you will benefit greatly from this book. I hope that it brings joy to your life because your joy will also be mine.

INTRODUCTION

Financial freedom is like any other freedom and must be available and accessible equally by everyone. The information must not be restricted only to the selected few, and we don't have to pay a fortune to acquire it. That's the premise of this book—to share with you the proven wisdom to achieve your financial freedom. How do we know it works? Because what I'm sharing is an accumulation of tried and tested financial wisdom coming from people who have walked down the same path. We may walk somewhat different roads, but we all share the same principles, and we all eventually converge at the same destination.

Why am I sharing this? Because I practice what I preach and know to be true—that wealth is unlimited and the joy of this wealth is meant to be shared with everyone. Wealth creation has long become a political game, and many keep it to themselves. They still live in the world of scarcity, believing that wealth is very limited and that they can never get back from the things they share. They fail to understand that the currency of love is superior to the currency of money. And wealth is indeed like love in one aspect in that the most ineffective way to get it is to ask for it, and the most effective way to get it is to give it out willingly.

Why another book on personal finance? Because there are only few that give us honest, complete, and practical information. This book is by no means perfect, and I'm not a guru. I don't want to give you false hope. I merely analyzed how successful people achieved their financial freedom, tested it on myself to see if it works, learned some things the hard way so you don't have to, filled in the gaps I found along the way, then compiled it in the most time- and energy-effective way in order to share it with you. I'm a living proof that these principles work, noticeably by the things I used in this book myself.

But let no one's word do the talking; let the wisdom that lies in the following pages do it. Talk is cheap, so prove it to yourself by acting on all this information *to the end*. Don't stop half-way through and be a sour grape. You must follow this book sequentially and completely. The book has been designed so that you'll derive the most benefit if you understand one part before moving on to the next for each part completes the other.

Part I will cover the most important aspect in our journey toward financial freedom, our mind-set. Part 2 will explore the strategic tools of becoming financially free. Part 3 is where we apply these mind-set and strategies into our real lives. The Q&A part will cover some of the financial questions people often ask me.

You cannot read this book once. There are too many things you will miss on your first read. The simplicity may give you the illusion that certain parts of this book are not as important as you may think, taking for granted the effort to simplify what is otherwise very large and complex information. But on the same token, throw away the idea that in order for something to work, it has to be complex. The truth is simple and it works.

The information has also been summarized so that you can read it in a single sitting, but the impact will be for a lifetime of an exciting adventure. Never ever forget the fun part of the journey as we discover ourselves on our way to financial freedom. And when you've reached that elusive financial freedom, it becomes your responsibility to share it with others. Only by sharing can you truly become wealthy. It is because of others that one can achieve financial freedom, so remember them when you're at the top. Your achievement is not measured by how much you've taken off this world but by how much you've given away and done for others.

I sincerely wish you the very best for the journey ahead.

To everyone's abundant life, with love,

Andrew Jevon
Perth, Australia
January, 2012

THE MIND-SET OF FINANCIAL FREEDOM

This is where it all starts and where it should never end. Getting the right mind-set is the prerequisite of financial freedom. Financial freedom is a result. And result comes from cumulative action, cumulative action comes from decision, decision comes from unbreakable belief, unbreakable belief comes from rational thinking, rational thinking comes from idea, and your idea comes from your mind-set. *Everything begins in the mind.* Our mind-set is what drives us from ignorance to understanding and wisdom. Our mind-set is what propels us from knowing to doing and persisting. How you think really determines your life and who you are. It will make you or break you.

I can start by giving you all of the so-called secrets to various wealth-creation strategies, but without the right mind-set, you will only know more, but you will not do more. Worse, you might think that it's too complex and you give up at the very first sign of difficulty, or you'll just keep it for tomorrow, when the time is 'right'. Getting the right mind-set is about going to and addressing the root of the problem.

The ability to act and act properly upon knowledge is an ability in its own right. And the mastery of this ability is what separates successful people from the population. Make no mistake; this is the most important part of the book. Your mind-set is the source of your wealth. Prosperous people have a prosperous mind-set, so they attract wealth and opportunity.

Violation of this mind-set will be the source of your future failures. Ignorance of this mind-set is the source of your past and current failures. Don't learn the hard way and think that mind-set has less value compared to technical advice. The result speaks for itself.

So you must understand, continually be reminded of, and practice the following mind-set. You must embody and learn to integrate this mind-set as part of your character. Focus on it, and once you get your mind-set right, you'll notice that wealth will flow in seamlessly.

❖ **Have an open mind. You must be willing to accept what may not be your comfortable thinking but proven to achieve results.**

Frankly, being financially free is simple in concept, but it is definitely not easy in the execution. And the steps involved may be against your conventional thinking. The fact that only few people are financially free points out that they understand and do something many don't or don't want to accept to be true. We tend to think that we know enough, but the result speaks for itself. Our place in life is the real indicator whether we indeed know enough. On the same token, we also tend to avoid important subjects we don't like. But as long as we are running away from it, we will be forever trapped in ignorance. And ignorance is usually the biggest hurdle in our path to prosperity.

So let's start by humbling ourselves. *We don't know what we don't know, and we don't know everything.* Be open-minded to new ideas introduced here and be sensitive to old ones we've always known. There may be concepts we never heard of. Or maybe there are old concepts that we remember by hearts but we don't do. Maybe because we think it's too menial, it doesn't interest us, or we think it won't help us where, in fact, it's where we're lacking all these times. The point is, we have to be willing to ever learn, to ever try what we've learned, and to ever figure out which works and which doesn't.

We also need to be open-minded because change is the only permanent thing in life. Either be with it or be left behind. Change is here to stay and no one can stop it. But that is good news because change brings constant and equal-level opportunities. So instead of avoiding it, let's embrace it and use it to our advantage. Be courageous because we cannot afford not to. *This age is the age of risk; the age of failure by ignorance, and the age of success by risk management.*

I recommend every one of us to think for ourselves and think critically what follows in this book. Test it for yourself whether it works or not. You don't have to buy everything what one person says, including mine. But I want you to give me and yourself a chance. The truth works. And that's the only way you can find out.

❖ **Financial freedom is not for everyone. Those who want it may never have it. Those who are able may never have it either. But you'll never know until you try it.**

It is not because we cannot learn the skills needed, but because some of us refuse to even consider the idea of it. *The body is capable, but the mind disagrees.* Success is more about mental attitude than mental capacity. I don't want to overinflate your confidence, but it is a simple fact that most of us have the capacity to LEARN to be financially free because it is definitely not a talent you were born with. You do need a talent to stand among your peers, but we're not here to do that. We are only following principles of success, and it is much less about talent and much more about your character.

When we're so used to seeing things a certain way, it is hard to look at them in a new, and sometimes better way. And it is often hard to accept the truth when the mind has been fed by lies over time. There are people who think careful investments are riskier than holding on to all your income from one source, one job. There are people who think a relatively smaller cost to pay now to avoid larger cost and to receive larger benefit later is a bad idea. There are people who are not comfortable with receiving money passively because they don't feel they have earned it. There are people who think money is evil without acknowledging the abundant evidence when money is used for a good cause for humanity. "A no is a no," they say. But behind all these, notice how *everyone wants to go to heaven, but not everyone wants to read the Bible from cover to cover.* Well, everyone is entitled to their opinion. But not every opinion is valid. I only ask all of us not to be so presumptuous on anything and find out for ourselves before making an informed decision. To me, trading time for money is very limiting. It pegs your earning capacity to the number of hours per day and forces you to delay what you would really love to do, be, or try in life.

Let happiness be your guide, not money or greed. If you know what financial freedom is like and you're not enticed by it or you are convinced that you won't be better off or happier by it, then by all means don't do it. Don't do something just because I or others advise you to do. Any kind of freedom is very personal and emotional. It is like deciding to buy a home, to get married, and to have kids. No one should tell you to do any of these. Do it because you want to do it, not because of what others want you to be and do. You only live once, so you better get the best out of it by yourself.

But happiness alone is not enough. Your happiness must be anchored with your purpose. You have to know exactly why you want this. *You have to know why you are not going to give up along the way.* And treasure your purpose because if you know the reason why you're fighting, your motivation will fuel you through the end, even though you may suffer setbacks along the way.

And remember this, *no one can motivate you. You have to motivate yourself to achieve what you want in life.* At the end of the day, it goes back to you. The gurus cannot do YOUR work and can only inspire you. *Never let anyone motivate you. If you're motivated by others, you'll have others' motivation in you, and it won't provide you enough fuel to run through the darkest hours ahead.*

I'm not a guru who pumps you with overinflated confidence, which will be very damaging when you will eventually face a temporary setback. Overconfidence can be worse than being a pessimist. I just sincerely want to empower you to acquire the necessary knowledge and mind-set to create the life you wanted, so you will be self-motivated and you will soldier on to the end. I'm not empowering you based on false hope, but based on the fact that you're able to do this. I've studied many successful people, and they are no different from all of us. Some are even starting out in way worse and tougher conditions than we can imagine.

But first, I want you to understand that in reality, *knowing or imagining something is not the same as experiencing it.* In my own personal journey, my expectation of the difficulties and the successes were not the same as the reality. Chances are your real success may or may not exceed your expectation, and your fears may or may not be justified in real life. But the point is, you cannot let your fears or your limiting self-beliefs deny you what you are entitled to.

Understand also that it has much less to do with your looks, education, background, intelligence and, whatnot, but much more about how you view yourself and the world. You don't have to be a genius. The world is filled with geniuses, but not all of them are financially free. *So don't worry about things you don't have now because you already have what you need.* Not in the cliché meaning, but in the fact of possessing the brain and the body capacity to do this. However, it's up to you whether you want to use it or not. *It is solely your decision, not your condition, that determines your life. And remember that there is always someone worse than you overcoming things worse than what you have.* If people with less talent and less favorable start can do it, try finding out the rational reason why we can't do it too. We won't find it, unless we create one perfectly suited for the comfort of our own reasoning.

Yes, the journey toward financial freedom is filled with hard work, smart work, sacrifice, calculated risk, courage, and commitment for at least the first few years. You will be forced to change, to do things you don't necessarily like, to meet people you don't necessarily feel comfortable with, and to be out of your comfort zone. But you will be able to enjoy the fruit of your labor too, which will always be greater than the cost to acquire it.

At the end of the day, it's about your life, which is way more important than anything. So as long as you protect the important things first, you can invest your way to financial freedom with peace of mind.

❖ **It's not about money. It's not about being rich. We have to stop monetizing everything.**

There are many things in life that come with a price tag, but there are countless things money can't buy. True, money doesn't make us happy. We really need a holistic wealth to be happy, and there are many miserable rich people out there. But let us not be hypocrites and accept that we need money to survive, and money does give us choices in many areas, flexibility in lifestyle, and has a great potential to share happiness around. *Wise pursuit and proper use of money is not evil; laziness and finding excuses not to pursue wealth for the greater meaning of one's life is.*

Money must only be used and regarded as a mere tool, and nothing more. But it's a great tool indeed. If we need to nail down something, a hammer would do a better job than our bare hands. But never ever forget the fact that it is only a hammer and nothing more. It is a dead object that must be used to serve us and others. We must never put more value to it than it deserves. We must never be the slave of it. The most dangerous mind-set we can have is when we think money has priority over our life or others' lives. You and the people you love must come before money. Only then you will have the right mind-set to seek and to keep money.

Financial freedom is also not about being rich. Being rich is not the goal. The goal is to ensure that you and your family are free of financial pressure and that you'll have more time to take care of important things in life. Being rich is totally subjective. Greedy billionaires can easily say their money is still not enough. Besides, if you're rich, the temptation to lose yourself will be so great. You may sacrifice and lose your integrity for the sake of a massive gain, and integrity is actually one of the main ingredients of financial freedom. The temptation to create profit out of nothing can be hard to resist. We will also be much more attached to our money, and we'll be giving it more value than it deserves. We will never find peace and wealth because there is simply no amount of physical money that is enough.

Greed is a product of the mind, and no physical money will ever satisfy it. No amount of money will ever make us wealthy. We must accept this now, or we'll learn the hard way. On the other hand, wealth, being also the product of the mind, can be satisfied even without the possession of physical money. At the end of the day, how we view ourselves and the world is what matters. *The truly wealthy is the one who is content with what one has. To seek wealth and have the self-respect and courage to say enough.*

It is totally pointless to have all the wealth in the world but we pay that with our own life. And be aware early on that there is no such thing as an instant or quick rich scheme. If you do get it quickly, you'll lose it as quick. If you have never been to a gym and you're suddenly given the heaviest dumbbell, you'll break your arm before your first rep. Having a million doesn't automatically make you a millionaire. You have to be prepared to be financially free. The good thing about doing it relatively slower is that you'll grow with your wealth. And because your wealth will not accelerate as fast, you will have more time to digest things.

Aiming to be rich also makes the whole affair looks unbelievably big. We're aiming to go to the moon without even having the knowledge to create a spacecraft. We'll give up before we even start. Financial freedom, however, is relatively easier if compared to an unhealthy ambition of wanting to be rich. *Don't seek money; seek instead a wealthy life without fear of lack of money.*

I can understand that money is emotional. And it is indeed a serious matter. Lack of money often takes its toll in one's health and relationship. And I can understand the terrible feeling of not knowing how to pay things for today and tomorrow. But often the emotion is attached to the physical money instead of what the money can provide us. *So detach yourself from money and attach yourself to wealth.* If you're saying to yourself, "I need money to provide for my family," then the emotion and the wealth should be attached to your family, not the money. Only then will you depart from the point of wealth and rationality in order to think clearly about how to get more money. You're giving your mind a chance for its full potential to solve money problems instead of exhausting it all to serve your emotional roller coaster.

Money doesn't solve money problems. Without financial wisdom, more money only creates more demands and problems. You'll automatically and unconsciously learn very rapidly to spend the extra money, and you WILL have a reason to justify it. Money without financial wisdom is money soon gone. So even if someone gives you money to clear all your debt now, without the right mind-set you will get into debt again.

The solution lies in becoming a holistically wealthier person, learning how to better manage your life, and therefore, your money. And that decision lies entirely in your hands.

❖ **At the end of the day, it's about you. To be something or to be nothing. It's your choices, your attitudes, and eventually, your life. You can choose to think and act positively, and you can choose to think and act negatively. Either way, you're right, and you will live with the consequences of your choices.**

You have a choice regardless of where you are in life. No one else can do it for you, especially the choice in your thoughts. Your thoughts determine your belief system, your action, and eventually, your life. Doing nothing is also a choice, and it will also eventually determine your life. So come to think about it—*a choice is power.* A large amount of scientific literature has been published on the supernatural power of our mind. It is the ultimate personal leverage—*using your very powerful mind to propel you to success.* And that power lies solely in your hand. It's your choice to put, or not to put, or to let someone else put things in your mind. The control is in your hand. It's not easy, but you can start to critically think things you hear and see. In any situation, it's our choice whether to think ourselves as victims or victors because they both are equally valid. Sadly, most of us will never get a chance to fully appreciate the immense amount of wealth we already have.

So let's start with our choice of thoughts because this will directly determine our success. *The aim is to create positive thoughts that will maximize our chances to create positive actions that lead to positive results.* In order to do that, we must first of all cleanse our mind from negative thoughts. It is not going to be easy because *negative thoughts generally seep in secretly without our consent, and we subconsciously and habitually allow it to be rooted so deeply it provides a challenge on itself just to remove it.*

We are the end result of our mind programming, but it is often not programmed by ourselves. For the better or worse, we are who we think we are, what we were taught to be, what people told us to be, what the society shaped us to be. *So stop being what others want you to be, and start to be what you want to be. Transform yourself from restriction to freedom, from discouragement to encouragement, from wishful thinking to reality, from lies to truth, from negative to positive. To not only knowing, but also understanding. To not only understanding, but also doing. To not only doing, but also enjoying.*

But why bother removing negative thoughts? Because they eat your soul bit by bit until you're spiritually crippled to attain any wealth, and that will be reflected on your physical life. It will be a massive hindrance on your path to success. Notice that miserable people have very negative thoughts, and they are consumed by it, not knowing that these negative thoughts are the very source of their miseries.

One of the easiest ways to acknowledge and remove your negative thoughts is to be open-minded and to receive understanding. Wisdom will prove to us that our negative thoughts are not accurate. In terms of financial freedom, there are lots of negative thoughts and myths that often sound like a good excuse, but very often, they are inaccurate. We will cover some of the most common myths of financial freedom.

- Myth: There are so many smart people or experts out there already; there is no way you can match them.

Fact: Every master used to be a disaster. No one was born great. You can be an expert yourself, but even if you're not, wealth is unlimited, and you just have to search for your share by accentuating your uniqueness. That is the best way to compete. Besides, the existence of others can only promote competition, which is good for the society. The point is, we have to do something to get a piece from this unlimited wealth. If we keep procrastinating, if we keep focusing only on counting how many experts are out there, if you keep relying and believing only others can solve your problems, then you are letting lies control your life.

- Myth: There is not enough resource for us anymore. All resources have been exploited by the rich. Even when there is a great opportunity, there is always someone who gets there first.

Fact: Rich and poor people all exploit resources. Human beings are the worst species when it comes to stewarding resources. We're on the same boat. But in the journey of financial freedom, we're not in the business of exploiting others. Leave those to the people who live in the world of scarcity, so you don't have to worry about this at all. Wealth is unlimited and you're in the business of providing and sharing wealth with others. And the main resource needed for that is love, and love never runs dry, unless we think it does. So even when a great concrete opportunity snapped in front of your eyes, the fact remains that it is a great lesson to learn, and other or even better opportunities are already waiting for you. Opportunities always self-create because change is constant and wealth is unlimited.

- Myth: To be financially free you have to suffer, sacrifice relationships, and sell yourself to your work.

Fact: I think that's what happens when you're NOT financially free. You suffer because you sell your quality time, your most valuable asset, for a small amount of money. You sacrifice relationships because you know money won't come in unless you work for it. So you work even on weekends when you know you're stealing your family's time. That to me sounds like you're selling yourself to your work. When you're financially free, however, you have all the time in this life to pursue greater things than money, like your passion, your spiritual relationship, and relationship with your family and friends.

- Myth: Rich people are evil. You have to be evil to be rich.

Fact: We have to know whether we are jealous of them and can only bad-mouth them so we can feel good about ourselves, or do we really know that some of them are indeed bad people. No doubt, there are indeed bad rich people as there are bad poor people. There are ways to be rich via dirty work, deceit, and exploitation of others. In the same way, murderers are often not billionaires, and jails aren't mostly filled with millionaires. The point is you can only tell a tree by its fruit. So stop judging people by their material wealth. Those who do speak a lot about themselves. And the thing is, you will meet rich people along the way, and they have a potential to be your partner toward your own financial freedom. So in the world seemingly filled with bad people, the best policy is to be the good one.

- Myth: It's easy for you to say it or to write a book about it, trying to make it look easy. In reality, investing is not only risky but also complex. Besides, my life has a 'special' case no one will understand.

Fact: You're right. It's not easy. But hey, there's nothing easy in this life, especially those things that are worth getting. Your job is definitely not easy. I was never employed to do easy stuff. If you want something worth it—let's not sugarcoat it—you must fight for it. History has a long record of those who have it easy, won't respect it and will lose it. Besides, you can only say investing is risky and complex if you don't know about investing and you're not managing your risk. And people always say that they are different, with different and 'special' circumstances no one can understand. It is actually because they are different that they can achieve financial freedom. No one in a totally homogenous population can achieve financial freedom. You're only special when you've achieved something not when surrendering to life.

- Myth: I don't know how to start a business or an investment. I was never a number type. It's still about the risk of losing things I love.

Fact: So is everyone else at the beginning, no exception. Nobody was born business savvy. They all either acquired it one way or another or hired someone who knows about it. If you can do your job, you can do your business because both are about getting knowledge and acting on it. The difference is: the world is very discouraging to proactive people who clearly have the potential.

They will tell you that any investment is risky so they will have less competition for themselves. But frankly, is it risky? Of course, just like having a job. Nowadays, you can get fired anytime if the business deems it necessary. That's risky to me. But once you've achieved financial freedom, you'll have multiple incomes, and you'll thrive on good and bad economic times. So even if one or two sources of income fail you, you still have the other to protect you. Risk is part of life. Don't avoid it; don't tolerate it; manage it. Risk can be significantly reduced if you know what you are doing. And ignoring risk will increase the risk of you losing things you already have.

- Myth: I don't have the talent, the intelligence, the background, or the leg up.

Fact: Neither did I. I'm a living proof that if an average Joe can do it, there is at least a possibility that you can do it too. I never received an academic trophy in my school life. The awards that I did receive came later on and were purely of hard work, which we all have control of. But I'll say it again: this has little to do with your background, and when you're about to do something new, your fears are often created by yourself and are not reflected in reality. Knowing and imagining are not the same as doing it and experiencing it. The perception and the seeming fear prior to doing it are completely different from the reality of doing it. You'll be surprised at how different the two are. My idea of business before doing it is completely different after I actually do it. I got some things right, some things wrong. But again, you'll never know until you try. Can you suffer loss? Can you fail? Definitely. To a certain degree you will. It's the cost and the part of success. But every failure is like your school fee; you're being taught a precious lesson. And because you actually experience it yourself, the memory is much longer lasting. Of course, if your ambition is to be the richest person in the world, you're putting yourself unnecessary and unhealthy pressures, and you will fail badly because your focus is on your money, not on your wealth, and money has a bad habit of giving you nasty surprises. But if you have a humble and realistic expectation, it really IS doable.

- Myth: I don't have time for all these. I work nine to five, often work late and my weekends are always full with social activities.

Fact: That sounds like how it was for me. And you're correct. You don't have time. Nobody has time until they create time.

Time is the only currency where you are on the same level as the richest person in the world. So if you hoard your time, leaving this matter until you feel like you're free, then you'll never get it done. What you can do is to create and prioritize a time. Commit to yourself that you will spend at least thirty minutes every day taking care of your financial affair and that this thirty minutes will take priority after your health, your family, and your job. Only then you will have time for it. If you budget your time wisely and stick to your budget faithfully, you will have time for yourself. It does require discipline, commitment, and dedication, but hey, you're not doing it for anyone else but yourself. The wins and the losses are totally yours.

That barely touches the real negativity out there, but I hope you understand by now that negativity is not accurate and is harming you, that it will block your opportunities. So first, stop being negative and replace it with positivity. From now on, when you see someone doing something you've always wanted to do and you say to yourself "I can't do it," the more accurate statement to say is "I don't know how to do it just yet," then think, "How can I do it?" Saying "I can't do it" is shortchanging yourself. And we are very often guilty of short changing our own intelligence and ability. There are way too many things that humans can do, including achieving financial freedom, than those things that humans genuinely cannot do.

It's all up to you and you alone. You will need others to succeed, but you are the more important aspect in this case. However, being dependable even for yourself is not easy. We often disappoint ourselves at our attempts to accomplish things that we know will be good for us. So this is where commitment kicks in. If you don't commit, you'll never be there. You need a solid commitment based on solid reasoning so that if somebody asks or you ask yourself, "Why bother?" you can come up with a solid reasoning in a split second that you will hold on to no matter what. For some, they say it's pain that propels them to seek a better tomorrow. That can work, but you don't have to be that drastic. Although if you're complacent at things, then you'll less likely to achieve anything.

So it goes back to the question, are you happy with the way things are now? I'm not talking about money. Let happiness be your guide, not your greed. What is happiness, you ask? There are thousands of beautiful, artistic definitions, and my simple definition may be different to yours, but from experience, *happiness is when you're capable to have the freedom to experience the joy of who you are, what you do, and what you have, and to share this joy with your loved ones and everyone because you simply cannot be happy by yourself. What good is the world if you don't have anyone to share it with?*

So if you are totally happy with your current life, then don't bother doing this. But can you be sure that you will be happy tomorrow? Being financially free doesn't guarantee happiness, but you will definitely have more chances to address things that do not bring you happiness. You'll have one less thing to worry about, so you can focus on creating a better future in your life. The choice, again, is yours.

Our world is much bigger than our imagination and too beautiful to be wasted if you work for all your life. The world is beautiful beyond words. It's the people who make it ugly, who lie to you that you don't deserve certain things. And this lie has become an epidemic. It is sad to see lots of people who die young, but they just don't get buried until they are old and physically die. They've lost the fire in their life and surrender their life to fate. They think working nine to five until they retire is the one and only way to live this life, shortchanging themselves of the countless beautiful and exciting possibilities ahead of their lives, which are meant to be theirs anyway. Delaying and denying the happiness they rightfully deserve. Imagine the love you have not known and shared, the characters you have not the privilege to get to know, the places you have never been, the senses you have not experienced, and the excitement you have not discovered. I'm not saying you will achieve all these once you are financially free, but you'll have more time to seek and enjoy the finer things in life we are supposed to enjoy anyway.

It's about your life. It's about being responsible to yourself and to your family. If we don't bother knowing how to better provide ourselves and our families, then we're not being responsible. If we don't bother knowing how to make ourselves and them less stressful and much happier, then we're selfish. If we purposely stay busy to avoid important things we don't want to face, then we're lazy. And this is definitely not the place for the irresponsible, the selfish, and the lazy.

Besides, you can no longer play safe and be at the mercy of life. Financial recessions and depressions are permanent features of our global capitalistic economy. It's just a matter of time until they hit us hard, again and again. Who can guarantee your job? It doesn't mean that owning a business is less riskier and guarantee anything, but those with multiple passive incomes have more control and more chance of benefitting from both up and down markets. Too many people are dependent only on one source of income. It is risky. You are focusing all your money-making efforts to just one source of income. You're putting all your eggs into one basket. Having multiple incomes is always better than just one, especially when they are passive incomes.

So the name of the game is commit or don't bother. Discipline is a must. You have to keep your hands on the steering wheel because you have to keep adjusting the direction of the car toward your destination.

If you have a problem committing, then you ought to look at yourself and reflect on what you really want in this life. We have to accept that if we want to get what we want in life, we have to work and be committed to it. This is not a place for half-baked committed people. *Less than full commitment is dangerous. You will do things halfheartedly, and it may give your more trouble than doing nothing.* You have to work hard. You must not complain about the price of your investment. You must think about the price you have to pay if you DON'T make the investment.

It is also your choice to seek or not to seek help from others. But not seeking help is a sign of arrogance. *Arrogance is a combination of ego and ignorance.* We think we know everything, and we think everybody else is inferior and would never be able to help us. Toss away the idea that you can pull this off by yourself. There is nothing shameful with asking for help. We humans are created for the mutual benefits of all. We're losers if we don't seek help and then give up and say, "Oh well, this ain't for everyone, they say." That is the saying of a sour-grapes at its best.

It is your choice to think that you can rely on someone else or yourself for your freedom. I'm not contradicting myself. You do need to ask for help, but you can't rely on anybody, not even if your pension is guaranteed by the government. Stop this entitlement mentality. The world doesn't owe you anything. It was here before you were born. So just because you've worked hard all your life, it doesn't mean you can blame the government for not giving you enough pension. Never take things for granted, and take control instead. We are entitled to certain inalienable rights in this life, but for someone else to feed us with a silver spoon until the day we die is not one of them.

It is also your choice to retain fear or to cure fear with action. Everyone in this journey has a degree of fear. It is different from one another, but I can appreciate the fear of the unknown is natural to all of us. So make it known. We cannot run from fear. Fear is a product of the mind and won't go away until you settle it. And it does take a higher intelligence for someone not to be biased and prejudiced on anything. It takes more brainpower to look at things objectively before making an opinion than just to assume. But the reward is higher too, and the benefit is all ours. Understanding and doing something will significantly remove the fear involved. At least try. Start small and dream big. I'm sure once you have experienced small victories, it will propel you to go all the way. Nothing replaces the transformational feeling from having a job to not worrying about money ever again.

On the other hand, people can also fear success. Funny as it may seem, but something that we really want, something we have been pursuing all our lives, may actually intimidate us when we are so close to it. We fear of being successful. We fear what other people will think of us.

Again, anxiety over something we don't know. Look at your purpose. I can understand your concern, but if you do it bit by bit, you'll grow with it and you'll know where the limit is and the point when you know you need to stop and refocus. If you do this subtly, if you don't show off, people wouldn't notice it. And you would be able to enjoy the fruit of your labor with peace of mind.

Finally, it is also your choice to start your journey toward financial freedom with a change.

❖ **Change starts from the inside. Your personal success is very influential to your professional success. You can only be successful when you've conquered your inner self.**

Inside every one of us lies our biggest enemy. You must defeat your inner conflict first before your outer conflict. Most of us have lost control of our thoughts and have never been taught to regain that control back. And sadly, instead of taking charge and being responsible for our own thoughts, we rather put the blame on someone or something when things don't go the way we want them to. Rather than working something out, we rather spend our energy being creative in making up excuses and blames. If you blame someone, you give that power of choice away, letting others make you feel miserable. Think instead, "I always have part in any of my successes and failures, so I will accept any of them as my own choice." Stop blaming and creatively creating excuses.

Our personal success has a connection with our self-image, our inner world. External forces can indeed hold us back or move us forward. But they are not as influential and powerful in reality as they are in our own minds. The power of self-belief is stronger than the power of what others believe about you. What you believe to be true about yourself is more important and way more powerful than what others believe you to be. This is why underdogs often win. They don't have the support of the crowd, but they are using the best resource available to themselves, and that is their mind. They believe they can do it; they don't believe or care when people say they can't do it. And that's what propels them forward and take the best action.

Only by honestly examining the internal forces can you begin to really control your present and your future. *Your self-image limits what you might attempt and what you might accomplish.* However, these are all acquired beliefs and learned behaviors. You can't outperform your self-image, but you can change it. You can experiment, test and push your limits. The way to uncover your own hidden talents and interests is simply to experiment. Instead of saying "That's just the way I am," say "I'll try that." *Limiting self-beliefs are beliefs that are purposely created by our mind to satisfy our fear but subconsciously sabotage our success.*

And when it comes to creating changes in your life, you cannot expect things to change by themselves. *You have to create and be the change in your own life.* How could we possibly expect something new and different in our lives without change? *How you initiate, react and adapt to change reflect your success.* Don't be scared and powerless of change. If there is something in your life that doesn't work, change it. Never ever let someone tell you a lie that something that doesn't work in your life cannot be changed; that life is but a destiny. *Each of us is given the free will at birth; don't ever surrender our biggest gift.* Think about your own life. How many times have things changed? You moved houses; you found a new partner, new goals, and new friends. In every one of these situations, your life is consciously and subconsciously changed. In the same way, you can change your direction today. You must believe that you can do this simply because it is a fact. Believe that financial freedom is possible, and it is possible for you.

Wealth has been created since the beginning of time. It's not new. It's definitely not out of reach. Success is not something mysterious. The information has been recorded in full and is accessible to those who seek it. *Success is the natural consequence of acting on principles of success. It is impossible and against the natural law to fail if you keep applying the principles of success while staying on the race.*

Let's hypothetically think that financial freedom is a product you can buy off the shelf in the supermarket. It is just a must buy; you know you want it. You've instantly come up with thousands of reasons why you must buy this product. But the price tag on it says, "Purpose, Discipline, Courage, Determination, Action, Hard Work, and Sacrifice." Would you buy it?

❖ **You will fail before and after you succeed. It comes in the package. There is nothing you can do about it. But there is something you can do when you're faced by it.**

Making an important decision is never easy, but that's barely the start. If you use your power of choice to decide to proceed, accept that you will fail before and after you succeed. Failure is part of success. Full stop. *You are not ready to win big, if you're not ready to lose a little.* Take it as a hard fact or make your own futile attempt to rebut it. We will all face temporary failure along our journeys. *Success is never a straight line. It's full of ups and downs and requires constant correction.* So it is better to be prepared than taking optimism to the unreasonable extreme. Not even the experts get it right every time. In the world of finance, there is no one person who has never lost money. Now, failures come in different shapes and forms and affect people differently, so in this case, we will be focusing on financial failures alone.

Don't kid yourself. Financial failures can be devastating. And lots of people fail and give up on their journeys well ahead of their potential. There are many who fail but they don't make as much headlines as the successful ones. I don't claim to know every cause of their failures, but the one cause that I do know is because the mind-set of wealth is not rooted in their thinking, and their emotion takes over. So let's first acknowledge that most people attach a subjective emotion into their financial failures. You must take out the emotion off your money and put it somewhere else worthier. *Emotion doesn't have a place in the investment world. Those who put theirs will surrender their wealth unwillingly to those who don't put their emotion on it.*

I myself was emotional. I thought to myself, "I've spent countless nights on my investment, I MUST be rewarded." I demanded fairness. I kept saying to myself, "You have no idea how much sacrifice I've put into this project." And the more upset I was, the further away I was from success. The truth is, nobody cares. Accept that everybody always asks, "What's in it for me?" So as long as you don't serve a purpose on what people want, you won't get paid a single cent no matter what, unless it is a charity work. This is what capitalism is all about. It works on the basis that we are all self-interested human beings.

Of course, losing $10 and $10 million is definitely not the same, but the approach to handle it is the same. Some may see it as the biggest failure in their life. Some think of it as just another day on the job and doesn't sting much despite both having lost the same exact amount of money. It's how they prepare, see and respond to failures that matter. And it takes guts, patience, and a great attitude toward failure to succeed. I honestly learned much more from my failures than my successes.

Take another perspective. This is the truth: losing money is never as painful as losing your loved ones, which cannot be valued or replaced by money. So if you play it safe, you really only lose what is replaceable. In the game of money, people constantly win and lose. And history is filled with people who have lost so much, and not only did they have the courage to start over, they learned from their mistakes and rebuilt their wealth even more. So if we prepare ourselves well and have the discipline to protect ourselves and our loved ones first, then it's not risky, and failures will not knock you down flat.

There is, however, one very thing no guru has ever thoroughly addressed in my journey so far—*failure sucks, big time!* Especially when you don't know how to handle it. I'm not going to sugarcoat it. We all know this. Failures in life hurt physically, emotionally, and spiritually. And sometimes for a long time. You feel grief, regret, and just plain pain. And I really don't appreciate it when people say motivational things to my face in my darkest hours.

I don't appreciate it when I'm being compared to others who have lost even bigger things in life. Well, although it is right, I'm not like them. I can never be, and I never want to be like anyone else. An original always has more value than a copy; why should I want to be like anyone else?

And these so-called gurus give funny advice, which just doesn't work when you hit rock bottom. No matter how many great uplifting quotes you remember, no matter how deep you anchor your good feeling, they are almost practically useless in your darkest hours, especially if you are not prepared. I think they have lost touch that we humans are never immune to loss. So from my experience I can say that if you feel like crying, then cry. If you feel like sharing your problems, then share it with your confidant. But if you need to channel your frustration, then do it alone. Don't involve others. Don't involve alcohol and drugs. Frustration is a bad excuse to harm anyone else. If you feel totally dreadful one day, then give yourself a break. Forget everything and try to have a good night's sleep. Things always look better in the morning.

The point is *you to have to have the advantage of being prepared when dealing with setbacks. Prepare your failures ahead of them.* You have to expect and prepare for setbacks. If you haven't and you fail, then you have no choice but to take your time during your failure. Wait a while until you can rationally think that those losses are not as big as they were when they happened. Don't wait too long though. You'll be tempting fate to take over your life. You'll start to find excuses not to get up again. You'll become lazy. Remember, dreams are created in the heart and minds, and there your dreams can die.

I pray and hope that none of you get dragged into a deep failure to the point of numbness because you were not prepared. I do not want to claim or assume to understand what you have gone through, but I can tell you that had I had a better mind-set, I would've perceived it differently and wouldn't dwell on my failure. Once you understand the mind-set, you will see things differently. Instead of being angry, you will be in control. Instead of feeling like you have failed, you will know that you have learned something precious. Instead of being depressed, you will realize it is not you personally who fails, just your action.

Understand first that you are equally responsible for your successes as you are for your failures. That's good news. It means you are more in control, and you can directly influence the rate of your success and failure. So you must never feel ashamed for trying and failing because those who have never failed are those who never tried. At least you suffer and learn because you did SOMETHING rather than doing NOTHING and never learn anything, and then really fail in life. You must also understand that failure can never overtake you if your determination to succeed is anchored deeply within you.

Everyone fears of losing anything. Some problems and fears are real. No kidding. But we have to objectively find what the real problems and fears are. If you don't understand something, your problems and fears will look way bigger than they really are. The fear itself is natural and is not the problem; it's how you handle it. *Becoming a winner means being unafraid to lose, knowing your loss is not fatal to your life because you are well prepared to minimize it. Failure inspires winners, defeats losers.* Big and small failures are the moment you learn the truth about yourself. It's a great mirror. It's the moment you'll know whether you're a winner or a quitter. Each failure increases your chance of success at the next attempt. You will at least know one way of how not to do things. Use it to make you stronger and smarter next time. Turn every disaster into a learning experience and a lead to more opportunities. Remember also the old saying "This too shall pass." All the worldly things shall indeed pass. So just learn from your failures and from your past, but close the chapter. Remember your past achievements when you are about to give up and remember your past failures when your head is getting bigger.

Stop blaming. It is very tempting to blame your failure to someone or something. Creating a better future starts by spending less time in the past and taking action in the present. You must use this moment, the only time you have. Don't blame the past or worry for the future. *You must understand that your circumstances aren't you. Good and bad things happen, and you can't control what happens to you, but you can control your actions and your reactions. When you stop blaming, you take back your power, and you'll look at problems differently.* You'll be less emotional and can see rationally how things went wrong and how to fix it instead of being hostage by others because you keep consciously thinking that they are the problem and unconsciously thinking that they have the only way out.

Stop feeling sorry for yourself. Only losers do that. Your loss is never as bad as others. Let's move on. It may give comfort if we seek and get sympathy. Sharing your struggle is fine, but if we expect sympathy, we subconsciously think that our problem is bigger than us and subtly expect others to fix our mistakes. That's laziness. What you need is to forgive yourself and others, be responsible to fix what has gone wrong, then move on.

You must also cultivate the habit of laughter. Laughter reduces all things to their proper size. Don't take this journey too seriously. Enjoy today's happiness today. Happiness must be sown and reaped on the same day. Just like emotion, sadness and frustration are of no value in the investment world. However, smile and each kind word spoken from the heart can be exchanged for wealth. Remain as a child, who always looks up to others, and you will never grow too old.

The truth is, there are only two kinds of failures: the real and the fake one. The fake one is unjustifiable and should only be treated as school fees in life lessons. You don't achieve what you want, you lose money, you lose confidence, you deny your failures, you create excuses, you think you're just the victim and cannot change anything. Those are fake failures and cannot be justifiable. You only need to acknowledge, identify, take responsibility, fix, try again, try again with different strategies, learn from it, and avoid it. It is a choice, an exercise of your free will. Just make sure your failure is never wasted. The only time failure is wasted is when you don't learn anything from it. You don't write it down because you think you will remember it. You disregard it because you think the lesson is too menial to be remembered. *Remember that the only useful and positive thing that can come out of any failures is the teaching.*

The real failure is the failure to act and failure to act wisely. This is the worst of all failures. You may get one hundred rejections and one success if you act, but you'll get an infinite amount of rejections and zero success if you don't do anything. The real failure is when we do nothing, when we think we know everything, when we let people do our thinking, or when we think our fake failures are real. And real failure can often be the result of a repetition and accumulation of previous fake failures. That bad habit that accumulates, that negative thinking that accumulates, that poor choice with poor consequence that accumulates, that fear you ignore and amplified subconsciously, that thinking of doing the same thing but expecting a different result.

I'm not going to inspire you by saying success lies in the corner when you give up. The real success may still be far ahead when you give up, but one fact remains. Success is never attainable when you give up. Look at babies, and no wonder why anyone who can physically walk, walks today. They just don't give up no matter what. So if your financial freedom goals are humble and realistic, you do not have a reason to give up. You are unable to give up. There are millions of second chances, so persistence and determination are omnipotent. When you are about to give up, imagine letting everything you've built so far go wasted. Remember that if you play it safe, you've got nothing to lose and everything to gain.

So in any failures in the past, present and future, remember that it is the cost and the part of success. It comes in one package. You will temporarily fail. Emotion will destroy you if you use it. Numbers may change, but your psychology has to stay the same no matter how seemingly emotional it is. It sucks, but there is no way you can be successful without experiencing a drawback of one kind or another. *Failure is a price to pay for your success.* It trains you; it makes you wiser, but only if you learn something from it. Not giving up to failure is the only entrance ticket to the success club.

Failure rate can be greatly reduced with a good judgment, and you must develop and practice good judgment. It will not come to you unless you act and you get a direct feedback from your action. A good judgment is what separates classroom attendant from real-life participant. It cannot be taught by others; it must be learned by yourself. People can advise you on things, you can read books on it, but it is entirely up to you to filter things and whether to accept it and use it in your life as part of your good judgment arsenal. *Good judgment comes from experience, and experience comes from making bad judgments.* Again, this is why failure is part of the package. And that's why action is very important. You'll learn nothing if you do nothing.

But as always, be careful of what people say. I'm not contradicting myself. You need others' help, but you always have to absorb and filter what people say, and you alone should make the final decision.

❖ **Be careful of what others say or suggest to you. And be careful of what you say or suggest to others. Above all, choose your inner influence very, very wisely.**

Sincerity doesn't necessarily mean the truth. People can be sincerely wrong. Your loved ones wouldn't want you to suffer, and although their intention is pure, it doesn't mean they understand what you're doing. By now you should have a solid reason of why you want this, with a good judgment to justify it. Your loved ones probably wouldn't understand it, and they may try to discourage you. They'll ask you why you would jeopardize the security of your family by making investments. Well, the answer to that is we don't and we should never do. Your family should come before your financial matters. And you should be open-minded enough now to think that there may be a possibility to do this safely since there are so many people who have done it. Indeed, playing it safe means you prioritize yourself and your family first before you start investing.

We're social species. We gather around with those who are similar to us largely because we want to. We like the comfort, and being with similar people do give us comfort. We tend to share common words, thoughts, and actions with our inner circle. And you will also notice that as soon as you network with the people who are already where you want yourself to be, you'll think differently, you'll use new words, and you'll perform new actions. So this is a double-edged sword. Your inner influence is subtle but very powerful. Think how closely your outlook is with your parents', especially when you're young. You also tend to agree with what your teachers said. And in a harmonious relationship, you tend to be similar with your partner.

But you have to appreciate the fact that *you would never grow with a comfortable crowd.* Your friends are emotional to you, and I would never advise you to abandon them in your journey toward financial freedom, but you have to be aware that your air balloon will never lift off if the ropes are still attached firmly to the ground. And the more ropes there are, the more difficult it is to get the balloon off the ground. Some of them will think that you're endangering yourself, and they will try to "protect" you. Some will ridicule your attempt because they don't know what you know now.

In a way, they may feel their comfort is being threatened by you trying to move up the ladder. I'm not presuming your inner circle wouldn't support you, but look at their achievements and results. If they already have what you want, listen and think carefully of what they say. If they don't, then also listen and think carefully of what they say. One of the many ways to see someone's character and real intention other than to see their action over their word is to imagine whether they would still advise you the same thing and you'd still invite them to your home when they are stripped off their official position.

You need to be constantly positive and empowered in this journey because the journey isn't a walk in the park, and you will meet negativity along the way, so any internal negativity you currently have is really not needed. Be aware of their influence, distance yourself, and filter the negativity. Learn to say no, or they will think you're weak. The best thing you can do is to convince them, and turn them into your allies. You must do this at least to your close family members, because they will make you or break you.

Another strong influence is your outer circle, and it is not necessarily a person. In addition to what random strangers say to you, what you read on newspapers, what you see on TV, and what you see on the Internet influence you. If you keep reading negative newspapers, useless TV programs, and bad forums and sites, it will subtly affect you philosophy. The media and most people keep telling you that investment is risky and complex. They are still living in the world of scarcity. *The world is constantly trying to subtly influence your thinking to their benefit, not yours.* And the nasty thing about subtle influence is that it is often unconscious and repeated, allowing it to have a deeper impact than direct influence.

So never follow the herd. Think about the logic: just because everyone else is doing it doesn't necessarily mean that, one, you know what you're doing and, two, they know what they're doing either. Herd mentality is a double-edged sword, but more often than not, it is unproductive. I don't even want you to blindly believe in all the information contained in this book if others have read it too. This is not about me telling you what to do. This is about me sharing what works and empowering you to think and to do things for yourself. This is about you discovering yourself.

One sad fact I have to share with you is that not everyone wants you to succeed. Some would even want to hurt you so they would feel good about themselves. Most of us still live in the world of scarcity. They think that if you succeed, they will have less chance of succeeding despite of not doing anything themselves. The only people who will help you are either the ones who have a vested interest in your project or the ones who have pure intention to help. The very people who genuinely love you. And it can be outside your family and friends. Don't lose faith in people. Good people still exist, but they are heavily outnumbered by the not-so-good ones. Am I not contradicting myself when I say you must always think positively? Definitely not, but too much of a good thing can be bad, so you have to achieve a healthy balance of being positive, optimistic, and realistic. Like I've said, overinflated confidence can sometimes cause more damage than what being a pessimist can do to you.

It's really important to research everything thoroughly and to think for ourselves. Identify, filter, and think critically. Choose whom you want to be influenced by and whom you don't want to be influenced by. Don't be a cynic and a doubter; be a truth seeker. Cynics criticize; winners analyze. Be courageous and don't let rumors discourage you. In everything you do, either get a trusted source or find out things for yourself. Don't let the media do the thinking for you. Making your own decision, and then both enjoying the success and learning the setbacks from your own decision retain your dignity.

One more thing about your outer circle is that you must keep your journey a secret, or at least you don't actively tell everyone about it. People remember and will remind you of your mistakes and failures. And it is not a good feeling when others keep putting you down by reminding you of your failures. But if you don't talk openly about your journey and you fail, nobody will know, nobody will ridicule you. And if you're successful, you can just celebrate with your family and close friends. The whole world doesn't need to know about it. Showing off provokes jealousy. Don't be naive. There are people who think, "If I'm miserable, then everybody else has to be too." And they will not be happy if you're better off. Sadly, there are people who entertain evil thoughts on us if they think we're better off than them. A tough lesson in life is that not everybody wishes us well.

Besides, if you think showing off is good, then you don't have the right mind-set, and you're not fit to be wealthy. If your way to earn a deeper respect from others is by showing off what you physically have, then you're empty besides all your possessions, and you'll learn many things the hard way. Never allow your *stuff* to define you and control you. Don't use the money you don't have to show off to people you don't even like. Worst is using debt to fill your void, which will lead to self-destruction. If you let your possession define you, they will indeed be so.

If you're showing yourself as a millionaire, then you're just a millionaire and nothing else. Remember that you're on your way to being wealthy. If you keep showing off, you'll violate the mind-set, and you'll stay poor because *poor people are those who have lots of money but nothing else.* No morals, no conscience, and no compassion. You'll be focusing on things to show off and less on the wealth itself. So the rule is to keep your money discreet. Remember the old saying *"Better a little caution than a great regret."*

On the same token, just because you're financially free or on your way, it doesn't necessarily mean you can give advice freely to people. If you know exactly what you're saying, then it's totally within your judgment to share it. The thing is, even if you give the right advice, it doesn't mean they will use it the way you intend it, and you'll be the first person to be blamed. Again, I'm not contradicting myself. You need to share, but share it in a complete way so people can see directly how they will benefit from it. But in order to share, you have to have something they don't have, and that's why we need to educate ourselves first.

❖ **Wisdom is the foundation. Education is the door to your success. Action is the key to get through the door, but only positive and complete actions that count.**

We will cover true wealth wisdom at the end of this part. For now, let's focus on your education. There is a direct link between education and income and between education and opportunities; you cannot beat this system of life. Greatest wealth is not money but wisdom. *If you have wisdom, you can replace the wealth you've lost. But if you don't, even what you have will be taken off you. Knowledge is power only if used and used wisely.* So start by increasing your financial intelligence. If you don't know something, then find out what you need to know, seek it aggressively and make it yours *because where the determination is, the way can be found.* And the more you know, the more you know what to do, and the smoother and quicker you'll be financially free. Ignorance in this matter is very costly.

When you think about the cost of your education, think more about the cost of not being educated. Think of what's going to happen to you in years to come, with and without your education. The price of your education will be negligible compared to the benefits. And there is a massive cost in delaying or ignoring your education. It can potentially be the difference of leading a life of success and a life of failure. *Every single one of us will eventually pay for our education either the easy way or the hard way. Either we pay a little now or we pay a lot later.* That's because proper knowledge, which comes from those who have 'been there and done that', gives you a massive leverage. And without this leverage, you are making this life harder than it's supposed to be.

Education is about buying it once and using it forever. It saves you trial and error, and minimizes your risk. And education is an ongoing thing. Successful people are involved in lifelong learning. You have to be a lifetime learner. *The moment we stop learning is the moment we go backward in life.* But you cannot learn anything if you don't firstly know how to study. *You have to acquire study skills to get information from all sources quickly, and to organize and retain that information accurately, ready to be used whenever needed.*

But I'm not necessarily talking about going to a college because I've done it, and they didn't teach me how to be financially free there. Schools and colleges are systemic institutions to prepare students to be employees to earn income from their education, not to earn passive income from their investment and be financially free.

I'm talking about getting wisdom—to act wisely on what you know. Wisdom is superior to knowledge because being wise means not only you know the right thing to do, but you are also doing it because you know it is the right thing to do. If you use your knowledge for selfish or bad purposes, then you may be smart but you're definitely not wise. *Seek first wisdom because wisdom will turn knowledge into skill that produces result, turning knowing what you need to do into doing what you need to do.* Skills will save you time, help you make better decisions, and provide you with the benefit of a leverage.

Your education must also be holistic. *Little knowledge is dangerous. Either you commit or you don't do it.* Those with limited knowledge of investing can easily say the whole thing is so risky and they can easily fail when they take the risk of investing with limited knowledge. The one who knows the holistic approach to investing takes control and minimizes risk while enjoying a constant cash flow from their investments. And education is also personal. No one can put information into your brain without your own effort. We must accept that learning is part of our journey. If someone tells you exactly what to do, you won't understand it or remember it. You will devalue it and you won't learn anything from it. You must empower yourself. Nobody else can do this for you. I'm going to give you the rod, but you have to fish for yourself. If I only give you a fish, you'll be hungry again.

This is the reason why I only share to you what works, what to do, but not exactly what to invest in. One, there is no way for me to know your exact situation, and there is no such thing as one-size-fits-all system. If there are no two individuals with DNA alike, chances are they will think differently and they will do different things. Two, I will be assuming your preferences and making a decision for you, which is pointless. Three, it will be outdated by the time you acquire it. Four, even if it is not, you won't understand and won't learn anything from it, and therefore, five, it will be a disservice to you. Besides, people do not value free or easy stuff; it makes them lazy.

That is why in the financial world, there is a need for a personal adviser. It is prudent and it is a legal requirement for accountants and financial planners to advise you only after they have reviewed your situation thoroughly. But personal judgment is still needed because even if they give you a seemingly good advice, you have to understand the advice and know why it was given to you. *Never think that you can just pay someone and wash your hand and expect them to work your money to your best interest. Your best interest is often not theirs.*

Now, I don't claim to share with you all there is to know about financial freedom, but I can say that the information in this book should be enough to get you started, to get you investing, and to show you the path to financial freedom if you yourself choose to walk that path. As soon as you take care of the internal factors, the external ones will be easy to handle. As soon as you establish your vision, purpose, and strategy, getting and using information is relatively easier. You need theory, practice, and experience. I'm giving you the first two, but no one else can give you the last one. There is no magic bullet. No shortcut. No overnight success. No something for nothing. You must experience the journey yourself. Do not avoid difficulties. Look at problems as opportunities that lead you to sucess. Of course, there will be technical concepts, difficulties, and frustrations. Achieving financial freedom is not easy, but it is simple and doable.

Now without action, even proper knowledge turns into mere information. *Action separates those who look at life as a series of opportunities to be taken while the rest whinge and ask themselves, "What can I do? I'm but a victim." The difference of success and failure depends entirely on action. You act and take the chance, or you do nothing and the chance will be taken off you.* Action brings you to success and reduces the fear along the way. And fear often leads to procrastination. Tomorrow never comes, reserved only for the lazy and the unfortunate. Action also determines your value in the marketplace. Multiply your action to multiply your value. *It is better to act and fail than not to act and really fail.* Success will not wait. It will give what is yours to others if you don't act.

The only way to get you into action is to have a habit of action. There is no other way. You need to act repeatedly. Will power alone can only sustain you for the short term. Make it a habit. This is the hidden secret. It makes everything easier. *Success is a personality, a habit of living.* And habits are very powerful. Our lives are a reflection of our habits more than our education. And positive habits are powerful tools that can help you reach your full potential. Whether we like it or not, know it or not, *habits run our lives.* They have enormous hidden power. So focus on developing the habit you want. Make your habits serve you.

Take small steps to develop good habits. *They key is to identify your good and bad habits, then create good new habits to replace the bad habits slowly.* Bad habits are often unconsciously done. But don't just give up a habit; it's easier to replace a habit than getting rid of it because only a habit can subdue another habit.

Take action and confront your fear. Luck favors those who take action. Stop thinking successful people are there because they are lucky. They are prepared. So you need to *prepare yourself well and be on the constant readiness for action. Then take initiative to create your own opportunities, don't rely for others to give it to you.* Your fear will diminish as you achieve even small victories. And ignorance can only intensify your fear. If you leave financial troubles to a side now, you'll be hit hard when you are no longer able to do anything about it. The first step is always hard, the second step may be even harder. But you should know by now that hard work is part of the package, and it shouldn't bother you because the reward will be much bigger than whatever hard work you have to go through now.

Here's the secret to action: *Small actions, both positive and negative, accumulate and make a significant difference over time.* Take a step, a small step, every day. That's all this whole thing takes. Being financially free is great. And great things don't happen overnight. Thirty minutes a day doesn't sound much. But if you devote this to any particular subject, you'll be an expert of it within a year. But know this—*knowing and acting on what you know is not the same as focusing on it.* Where focus flows, energy goes. And focus is something everyone can do. You cannot do things just for the sake of it. You must be laser focused. When you're focused, you would be persistent and consistent to do anything necessary to make sure your action will produce the result you want. And once you have started and focused on your actions, there is something even more important. *You must finish what you start. One of the biggest failures in life is the failure to complete.* Many of us are great starters but poor finishers. We usually get excited by an idea, commit our time, energy, and money only to find the interest dwindling down along the way. *Successful people start at the beginning, never skip a step, only fast-track them, complete what they start, and start again and again once they complete something.*

❖ **You must start with the right philosophy and wisdom of wealth to be wealthy today and to be much wealthier tomorrow.**

By now you should appreciate that your attitude is everything. What you think really matters because *your actions are driven by what you most deeply believe about yourself and the world.*

Your philosophy is the key, in addition to your will power. Our attitudes change according to our philosophy. Our mind affects our lives directly. *How you view yourself creates your reality.* Success is a way of living. Successful people are successful because of how they look at themselves and the world. They have discovered something everyone is born with—*that we all have a conscious control of our reality. We are really who we think we are for the better or worse, consciously or subconsciously.* And your real philosophy—not what you say about yourself, but what you really do in life—is run by your subconscious. So be very careful with the control of your own mind.

Here's the simple formula of your philosophy and your life:

Your current mindset + your current plan + your current action = your current and future successes and failures.

Every financially free person starts with the right mind-set. So do what successful people do. Emulate them but never ever copy them or try to be like someone else because everyone is different. Think like they do. Pick up the clues they left behind. But at the same time put your stamp on your wealth. Your individuality makes you even wealthier because your value becomes irreplaceable. Everyone is different and unique. Accentuate your unique charm.

Psychology plays an important and fundamental role. Even when you're financially free, you may not feel wealthy because money is pointless without the psychology of wealth to support it. What we must do then is to start and depart from the point of wealth today! You'll have much less limiting beliefs and will be much faster to reach your financial freedom. *You must be able to enjoy what you have today to have more of what you enjoy tomorrow.* It's definitely not about faking it until you make it. It's about that genuine feeling. It's about knowing and accepting that you already have what it takes to be financially free. No one has it perfect, and God only gives each of us so much that our job now is to improvise and maximize what we have, as a test of responsibility. And we already have so much. If you keep complaining about things you don't have, the things that you do have will be taken off you.

Practice and start today to be genuinely wealthy. You must feel it and act now! "Someday" never comes. "Someday" does not exist. There is no perfect timing. No one knows tomorrow; someone's life and wealth can be taken off overnight. There is no perfect preparation. *Perfection is the enemy of success. Excellence in everything you do is the biggest ally of success.* Start now. Perfection and tomorrow never come. But being prepared and being excellent are what you can do today.

When you start today you will start to positively change your thinking, your behavior, and finally, your reality. Your choice of words will be different, how you interact with others will be different, and how you view problems in life will be different. And all these open up opportunities. It is only then that strategy and action can take place. Truly, there is no other time better than now because now is the only time you have. You can't change the past and you don't own tomorrow, not even the next hour. This moment is all we have. We can only learn from the past, live in the present, and plan for the future.

You cannot think you can only feel wealthy when you are physically wealthy because that moment will never come if you don't change your thinking today. *Don't wait to be wealthy. Start to be wealthy today because we all are wealthy.* Even a simple fact that we are alive means we have something money cannot ever buy, a pure invaluable wealth.

What is wealth? *Wealth is holistic and interdependent. Our wealth is the combination of all types of wealth and cannot be separated.* You have to address every type of wealth. You must not acquire one type of wealth and sacrifice or neglect the other because it will average out. A billionaire without morals, compassion, and integrity is poor. A financially free person but bedridden is poor. A perfectly healthy person but hated by everybody because of his or her selfishness is poor. The key is balance. Every aspect must be addressed constantly, and one must never overtake the other. These are the seven types of wealth.

1. Spiritual wealth. This is the wealth of the inner you. Once filled, it will pour into all other types of wealth. This is the most important wealth because *before someone is physical, he or she is spiritual.* As there are things seen, there are things unseen. How foolish it is to judge something entirely by how it looks, merely using one of our many senses. Someone cannot call us dumb just because they cannot see our brain from the outside.

This is what is considered by many as the missing link of wealth. And because it is not often addressed, we will cover it fully in the next section. For now, spiritual wealth is about connecting to our Creator, leading a life of integrity, honesty, humility, gratitude, compassion, respect, contribution, and celebration. It's about knowing and doing the right thing with the right motive. It determines how much real fun you have in life and how joyful the life you are leading is.

2. Physical wealth. This is the wealth in terms of physical health. How much energy you have every day, how clinically healthy you are, as well as your body capacity to experience wealth. In many cases, health is a choice. Lifestyle is much more important than genetics. Scientifically, DNA can either be improved or impaired by our choices despite inheriting whatever genes from our parents. So this type of wealth becomes important because if you have all the wealth in the world but you made poor choices and end up physically unwell to enjoy your wealth, then you're not wealthy.

Health is multidimensional. Without intending to simplify a truly complex topic, physical health comes down to five things: our diet and lifestyle, our sleep pattern, our exercise level, our mind management, and our sexual practice. All these directly and permanently affect our well-being.

3. Emotional wealth. This is your ability to handle emotional things in your life. Emotion is the fuel of life. It's about knowing why you do the things you do, controlling and mastering your own mind, accepting who you are, knowing how to manage stress, knowing how to get rid of emotional scars, and minimizing your chances to fall into an emotion trap again. It's about having a stable emotion, blending in rationality and good judgment, although by no means your life should be predictable and boring. But if you are unstable emotionally, you're risking yourself in anything you do.

4. Relationship wealth. This is how you relate to yourself and to the world. It's about giving and receiving love; developing healthy, real, and loving relationships. Love is the most superior currency. It is very satisfying to the soul to be at peace with yourself, to have meaningful relationship with someone special, with others, with nature, and with our Creator. It's about being honest and being yourself. How much do you care about the world, and how much does the world care about you? How good do you live your life? Because life is all about relationships.

5. Quality-time wealth. This is about mastering the gift of time, living and spending your time successfully. This is one the most important things in life. Your biggest asset is quality time in the form of life. Only when you have quality time can you enjoy and share the good things in life. Time allows you to learn, to earn, and to live.

If you don't master time, you'll have a hard time mastering anything else. Manage it wisely. Prioritize your time because there are many distractions on your way. Use it in a healthy way for yourself, your family and your friends. Mastering your time is also about not trading your time for something of less value but having the option to give it because you love to give it. Time is emotion, not just the quantity, but the quality of it too. If you have years in your life but spend it solely for the purpose of seeking money or spend it in jail or being sick, then that is not wealth.

Money lost can always be replaced, but lost time can never be recovered. That's why you can't be greedy; time wasted on recovering loss from greed is a bad use of time. We have to instead use money to buy us time. This is why money is a great tool. You can pay someone to do the menial and time-consuming things so you can focus on other more important things. Think of what we are really busy with. Where do we invest our times in? Oftentimes, we spend big on little things and spend little on big things.

Only God knows tomorrow; all you can do is to make every day the best day of your life. You spend one day, and you'll have one day less. One of the biggest surprises in our life on earth is its brevity. Your life is measured by time. When you waste time, you destroy life. You're in serious lack of quality-time wealth if you waste a day of your life and you think no harm is done. A day is very expensive because you only have so much. Cherish each hour, for it will never return, and its value is beyond price. A dying person cannot purchase another breath for all his or her riches. Do not kill time anymore. Procrastination must not be in your vocabulary. The joy of procrastination can never heal the pain of regret. And be careful, for regret can often be an unbearable, haunting pain.

6. Career wealth. This is your vision and mission in life. How happy you are with what you do and what you're going to do in life. Where you are in terms of doing things you are really passionate about. It can be working for someone else or working for yourself, but this is how you view the big picture, not your daily job description. This is about the answer to the question of: Do we go to our jobs for the money, or because our bosses tell us to, or do we go to our jobs to fulfill our missions in life?

7. Financial wealth. This is the amount of worldly belongings that is enough to support your other wealth. It is not worth it if you don't have other wealth. This is worldly possession, and this is why people often get it wrong. Instead of addressing our internal wealth first, which is much more important, we go straight to our possession and wonder why we are not happy by possessing all of them. *If you are not happy on the inside, there is nothing on the outside that can make you happy.*

How wealthy are you?

Now that you know all the types of wealth, let's make an audit of yourself. Rate yourself out of 10 on each type of wealth. Know which you are lacking and which you have an abundance of, then get an average score. Find out and see clearly how all your wealth is interdependent.

It's good to know where you are and where you want to go. But mind you, all these descriptions of wealth are ideals, so don't think you have to get 10/10 objectively on all types because nobody can. One, it is impossible. Two, only destructive greed can drive you. Three, even if you objectively make everything perfect, what is there left to do? What's the point of living then?

Everyone slacks from time to time; that's okay. That's part of life. No one is perfect. But make sure today is always better than yesterday, and you're ever onward toward your holistic wealth. If you subjectively feel like 10 in every aspect, then it is terrific. The scores are meant to be subjective anyway. A less fortunate person would probably rate you higher than you would rate yourself, but it is still a good exercise. Keep doing it as you go along and notice how it will grow as you grow.

The Model of Wealth

Here's a simplified model to achieve any types of wealth.

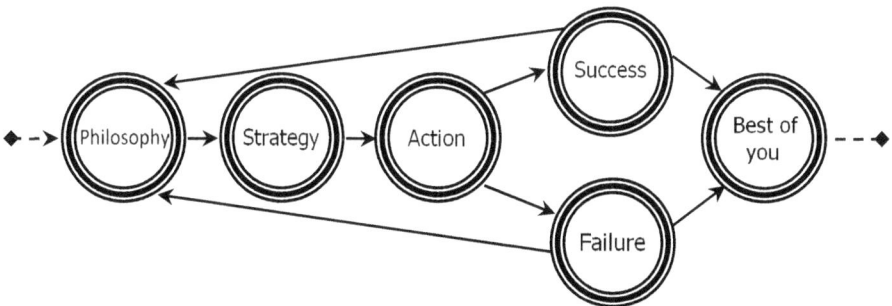

Notice and understand the following observations:

- In anything in life you want to pursue, it starts in the mind, your philosophy. You need to know what you want, why you want it and what you will offer in return. So notice that your wealth depends entirely on you alone. Although you will need the help from others, managing your philosophy is the only thing that you alone have full control of. All assistance can only come when you've pulled your own weight.

- Once your philosophy creates your goals, you need to create the strategy to achieve them. Not a simple strategy, but a concrete, written, smart, and achievable one. You need to find out how to get the best strategies, and then you seek them and you don't stop until you get them.

- Once you understand your strategy, your philosophy has every reason to act on it. And once you act on it, you will be faced with two possibilities resulting from your action: success and failure. Success is a natural consequence of consistently *applying* the *mind-set* and *strategy* of success. But both success and failure are only creations of the mind.

- If you achieve success, no matter how small, celebrate it and treasure it because it will motivate you to go further, and lifts you up when you are facing a failure. And when you have achieved success, two things should happen. One, you learn from your success and upgrade your philosophy accordingly, creating a loop. Two, your success will lead you to becoming a better person, creating a loop.

- If you meet failure, then learn from it and also treasure it because it will humble you when your success tempts your arrogance. And after facing your failure, two things should happen. One, you learn from your failure and upgrade your philosophy accordingly, creating a loop. Two, your failure will lead you to be a better person, creating a loop.

- Notice that the aim is not success, and failure is not the end of the game. They are only part of the equation. But through success and failure, considering you have the right philosophy, you will become a better person. Success is subjective, but becoming a better person who is wealthier in all aspects of life is apparent, objective, and measurable. You may not be worldly rich, but you will be living a wealthy life. Both success and failure are just life lessons. *True success is when you become the best person you can be because you'll be wealthy in all aspects.* Not what we have, but who we have become. And that will solve your problems. You will become greater than your problems. It is about the character behind your achievements. If your aim is to just have one success goal, the question is then, and then what? But if your aim is to be the best person you can be, you'll be occupied for a lifetime. Success and failure are only states of mind. But a better person is real, evident by real wealth.

- Again, you'll also notice that it is an endless cycle. There is no end. It's a loop with the aim of constantly becoming the best person you can be. One success or one failure, no matter how big, doesn't mean you're done. Even when you've become a better person, there is always an opportunity to learn, to give, and to be even wiser. Your to-do list never ends.

Once you have focused and have enough wealth in one type of wealth, move on to the next. The moment we think we've done everything there is to it in this life, it's the moment we stop living.

- At the end of the day, the reward is your own full life. A life fully explored, a life well lived. So the name of the game is to be the best of you. *Don't just be yourself; be the best of yourself.*

❖ Embracing spiritual laws of wealth is the only way to get wealthy.

I'm committed to share with you the holistic understanding of financial freedom. So I'll give you the missing link from what most people teach about financial freedom. *True prosperity comes from proper dealing from the spiritual level, which will transform itself into the material world.* The understanding of this concept is the ultimate key to your prosperity. The lack of this understanding is the reason why people envision, wish, and visualize wealth but never receive it. The reason why everyone rejoices at the concept of unlimited wealth but never understands and receives a share of it. The reason why everyone rejoices at the concept of us having all it takes to have whatever our mind desires but doesn't make us happy. The reason why we are wishful of the possibilities of our desires being fulfilled in the physical world but not understanding the spiritual source of such desires to make it physical. Make no mistake, just as there are physical laws, there are spiritual laws of wealth, and it is of supreme importance. You may not believe it, but it doesn't need your belief for it to exist. It works regardless, so might as well use it to our advantage. And once you embrace and practice the spiritual laws of wealth, you'll find it easier to find all other wealth.

We have to make integrity, compassion, and humility our cornerstones in life. These characters are very attractive to wealth and they have always been and will always be the foundation of success in anything in life. They may say business is all about transactions, but if you're in it for the long term, there is much more than that. You may be able to trick someone once, but you can never ever be wealthy by doing that. *There is only a win-win or lose-lose situation and nothing in between.* When we lose our integrity and compassion, we're exchanging menial short-term gain for long-term pain. So be honest and be fair in every of your dealings. Don't worry about those who don't; they disrespect and are unaware of universal justice, and they will reap what they sow either in this life or in the afterlife.

Indeed, wealth attracts wealth. *If you're a good steward on little things, you'll be given more. If you're a bad steward even on little things, what you have will be taken off you.* You must be wealthy first to get financially independent. And how you identify your wealth determines your wealth.

The positive feeling, emotion, philosophy and sense of abundance will make it easier for you to get the real wealth. You will not be in fear or negative mode. It will carry you through the hardship in the process, and you will operate from gratitude, not fear. Associate and accent the wealth you have already owned and be grateful for it.

And because you are already wealthy, you must start by sharing your wealth. It's a simple fact: *one can only give if one is wealthy.* So when you give, you ARE already wealthy. *And you must give first before you can receive.* We have to stop thinking of scarcity and stop thinking of getting for ourselves alone. Life supports life who supports life. So share love and wealth. Love eliminates suspicion and hate. Love protects you from adversity and discouragement. And to give is always better than to receive because when you give, you make God in the position of debt. And you can never out-give God. Make no mistake, the way you treat others is the way you treat God. God is not only in heaven but omnipresent, even in the ugliest slums of the world. So never think God doesn't know what you give out willingly even in secret.

When you give, you're seeding for yourself to reap in the future. You'll be more when you give. If a granary is kept filled with food and the food is never taken out, the food will turn rancid and it will destroy the granary itself. But if there is a cycle of giving and taking, there will be a need for a second granary. Make sure that you give with the right motive in the spirit of togetherness because if you are motivated only by your selfish purpose, your gift becomes useless. You'll notice that no matter how much you give, you are still not happy and wealthy. So you must give in the spirit of service and sharing. The good news is love is not about just merely giving to others. As you give to others, you give to yourself. Giving is a joy and a blessing in itself; it doesn't always have to be repaid by the recipient for you to benefit.

Positive thinking is an absolute must. Optimists often perform better or even outperform themselves. They have more chances of success. You must be positive to build a psychology of resilience and you'll think you're bigger than any problem. I don't believe in New Age movement or the so-called the Secret, where you can just focus and visualize something, then your wish will magically appear out of nowhere. I've tried it myself, followed the system through completely, but it didn't work. At first I thought this was just wishful thinking, but I opened my mind and gave it a go. At the end of the day, I was right. I was trying to use the system to create my own financial freedom. I didn't get a cent out of it. I discovered that the whole concept is only a fraction of the complete system of wealth-building. Wealth is holistic and when you only focus on one part of it, you will be disappointed. And focusing on positive thinking alone is very counterproductive to what you're trying to achieve here.

But there is a scientific explanation to how positive thinking invites blessings. It works by changing how your physical and mental senses interpret information. It will open up opportunities you won't get if you're negative. How? *Regular and purposeful affirmation scientifically change our subconscious mind, to the better or to the worse depending on the nature of the affirmation.* The evidence is so abundant in scientific journals around the world. So when your mind-set of wealth has taken over your mind-set of scarcity, you will see the world in a different set of spectacles, and you will spot wealth easily. When you have the mind-set of scarcity, you can easily find bad things in this world. In the same way, when you have the mind-set of wealth, you can easily spot wealth that your eyes were just oblivious to previously. So get a habit of thinking positively in everything you do in life, added with a little touch of reality.

Be grateful for everything in life. Purposely enjoy every moment of our breath. In life we tend to lose those we love deeply but are not grateful of. You must be thankful. Give thanks. Being alive alone is enough for us to be grateful. If we're not grateful for things we already have, which are a lot, there is really no point of anyone giving us more. If you've just given your friend one of the best gifts in the world but he or she couldn't care less about it, frankly, you would be inclined not to give something better next time, knowing it wouldn't make a difference. But if the gift comes with appreciation, you would be inclined to give even better gifts next time. We often forget how being grateful increases our chances of maintaining our lives and happiness.

There are so many things to be grateful for. Always look for reasons to be grateful. There are so many things you didn't help create but you enjoy. So be content with what you have. *It's always easier to look up than to look down.* If you are constantly comparing yourself with others who may be more successful, then you're trying to be a copy of someone else instead of an original of your own. Save yourself from an endless frustration of trying to be like someone else. Look down, look at the number of people who are way worse off than you and think of what they don't have that you do.

And if life is a beautiful gift, what did we do to get it? What effort did we make to make ourselves born? What makes us think that we deserve such a priceless gift? Nothing. Therefore be generous because you have been given such grandiose generosity. Never take things for granted, be humble, and be grateful always. It is very arrogant to disregard and discredit God when we were born out of our power and will die powerless. God knows that life is beautiful and therefore He gave it to us. Question is, what are you going to do with it? Are you going to waste it, or are you going to appreciate it and live the best and all you can be? To fulfill all your possibilities, to know your limit and to stretch it, and to be the happy person God wants you to be.

We also often take regularity and normality for granted. We often forget the very fact that routines and normality require maintenance. On a larger scale, just because the earth turns consistently and precisely to provide you day and night, it doesn't mean nothing maintains it. On a smaller scale, just because you're doing a routine, it does not mean things around you need to support your routine too. If you go through the same road every day to work, the road itself needs maintenance. And it doesn't mean that what happens in the journey is always in your favor.

Every time you go out and get back home safely, millions of things must happen. You must not encounter a drunk driver, you must not encounter a criminal who is willing to take your life, and you must not meet millions of other possible accidents. All these for every second of your life. So every time you go home safely, be grateful. Every time your kids come home safely from school, be grateful. Every time you take a shower and get out whole, be grateful. Every time you eat and you can taste it and digest it, be grateful. Every time you sleep and wake up again, be grateful. Every time you inhale a breath and still able to exhale again, you MUST be grateful. Every day, someone somewhere dies; their precious lives are taken away from them.

Being grateful guarantees your current and future happiness. How can you be miserable if you already have so much to be grateful for? *Being grateful tends to make you audit what you have, both internally and externally; both of which will open up opportunities and help with your positivity.* This access is not available to those who think they have nothing in life worth being grateful for, or have no one to be thankful to. The New Age movement always says to be grateful to the universe. Well, God owns the universe, so we need to thank the Creator Himself. *Gratitude must be directed toward something to be effective. Don't think that just being grateful to the void will do you any good. It is wrong and pointless to be grateful blindly.* God knows when you're grateful to Him or to the void. So those who blindly refuse the existence of a Creator will have a hard time becoming wealthy. They will not be supported by the source of wealth. And this is why people don't get result when they merely do what the New Age movement is telling them to.

We're living in the world where scientists receive an almost semi-God status in that once they are recognized as scientists, everything they say is what we believe in, no matter how absurd. Look, of course they know something we don't, but it doesn't mean we have to swallow their every word. Throughout history, scientists made as many discoveries as they made mistakes. We're now quite far away from the theory that our bodies are only made up of four humors, but mistakes in science are still made daily and oftentimes these mistakes cost people's lives. *Let their evidence speak for their science, not their words.*

Scientists offer you the evolution theory, which you'll know it is still scientifically unproven if you have studied it, that gives this selfish and romantic idea that no matter how bad you've become, no matter how many lives you're ruined, no matter how big the damage you've made in this life, you will not be liable for it because death will end it all. According to the theory, there is absolutely nothing after death—nil, zilch, pointless—because they believe in a religion that doesn't believe in God, accusing and assuming a lie that God doesn't exist. *But a lie—no matter the number of people who believe in it, be it the whole world—doesn't turn itself into a truth.*

Future scientists, with their advanced technologies, will laugh at our generation for believing a theory without scientific evidence. Up to now, there is no transitional fossil record evidence showing the progress from one inferior species to a more superior one, one step at a time. The very evidence they need to prove the evolution theory to be right hasn't been found yet, but many foolishly believe in it and worse, many base their lives on this unscientific theory. Just because they are scientists, it doesn't mean they know everything and they can't be wrong. Scientists, or anyone at all, can say something about anything. Talk is cheap. But at the end of the day, the evidence speaks for itself.

Evolutionists are still unsure of how life started on earth. What exactly causes inorganic chemicals to be organic? What exactly causes inorganic chemical to exist in the first place? What happened before the big bang? How did each species gain extra *good* genetic information to mutate and evolve to? How did various colors come into existence? How exactly did each species evolve to the next? They say everything came from one single bacteria, despite being unsure how this bacteria came into life in the first place, but how and who gets to decide which bacteria would become a tree, a human, a fish, an algae, or a bird in their future evolutions?

And when an anaerobic creature evolved to becoming aerobic, which organ came first to support the exchange of oxygen? The lungs first, or the nose? Or both? Where is the evidence when creatures were having extra but yet functioning lung tissue cells dangling inside their bodies while waiting millions of years for it to be completed and functional? And then wait for another millions of years to grow nose cells for external passage. What were the respiratory cells for while waiting for the external passage? Organs are complex and a quarter or half an organ doesn't make it functional.

How about digestive system? Did mouth and teeth come first, or intestine first? If it were the teeth, what were they for without intestine? If the intestine came first, what's the point of having intestine without a mouth? If they both appeared, that would kill the theory itself because it is too complex in terms of evolution to acquire such sophistication at the same time.

And if chaos theory is right, why do we have common organs with the same functionalities? Even taking into account rare physical abnormalities, everyone's eyes perform the same function. Everyone's heart pumps blood. Everyone's kidney is the same kidney bean shape. Shouldn't we have found a heart in the shape of a kidney, a heart which can perform the functions of the eye and a kidney which can pump blood? There is no such evidence today. And if the theory is right, why do we have common DNA with other creatures? Shouldn't our DNA have minimum commonalities just enough to point out that we all came from one single bacteria, and then we mutated chaosly and individually? And surely, if it is really random and chaotic, why are there only two sexes of human? If a random number can range from absolute zero to infinity with unlimited small divisions in between, why only end up with two?

And if life's purpose is to solely propagate, surely that will be the focus of our existence, and having just a single sex organ in our body would be counterproductive. Evolution should provide us with multiple sex organs for a massive and rapid propagation, yet one male finds the pillow more attractive than his sexual partner after propagation. Why are there still people today with genetic disability? If there is indeed survival of the fittest, there shouldn't be a place for love and sensitivity, and these genes should have been wiped out ages ago mercilessly. Yet love conquers even disability and people with disabilities still marry those without. It doesn't make evolutionary sense. If we really use our intelligence, there is no place for the evolution theory at all.

Evolutionists also don't believe in life's meaning. We will be very offended if someone says our lives have no meaning, yet if a scientist tells us so, we gladly accept it. Again, think for ourselves. If you have studied evolution thoroughly and have found credible evidences and a credible way to validate those evidences, then accept it as truth. In the mean time, blind faith and political agenda are the only ways anyone can accept evolution as true. Mind you, there is little pure science now and plenty of political science. Many scientists who use their intelligence to validate that evolution is unscientific and are therefore unwilling to compromise their intelligence, often get fired from their post as academics.

But pure science is never bad. It is the art of seeking the truth. Science has found that our universe has a beginning, and it will eventually end as it keeps expanding and losing energy. But science alone cannot tell us what happened prior to the beginning, why we are living now and what is going to happen to the universe after the energy is depleted upon full expansion. And why the fact that the earth is perfectly suited for life. There are things we do know as much as there are things we don't know. We have neither control nor knowledge of our arrival into life (prelife) and our departure from life (afterlife). We only have free will to decide where we are going to in this life and in the afterlife.

Science is now so advanced that it can sustain a dead body, keeping an empty shell until the body degenerates naturally. Scientists can practically create a simple zombie. They can open and close a dead body's eye via bioelectrical stimulation and do the same to move the arms and legs, but nothing more. The body cannot talk, think, or even walk. So something must be missing for this body to be alive, to express emotion. This is commonly called a soul. And a soul operates in a spiritual world. Anyone who has gone through a real near-death experience can tell the universal experience of knowing that death is not the end of everything and a soul is ever existing. Science has given ample evidences that lead to a conclusion that there is more to life than our physical world. And why do we even die? Evolution should have solved this problem ages ago. The genes that program cells to die should not exist in the first place or at least being wiped out to maximize our chances to ever propagate. Yet no human has ever escaped eventual death. So as there are physical laws in the physical world, there are spiritual laws in the spiritual world. And these laws have direct and significant impact on our lives here on earth.

And if there is a spiritual world, who runs it, who owns it, who has control of it, and who made it exist in the first place? If God doesn't exist both in the spiritual and physical world, then our lives on earth will be devastated. If there is no God, there is no meaning, no absolute value, no right and wrong, no justice, and no law. Indeed, why do we bother keeping our integrity, being honest and fair in all our dealings, especially in today's climate where businesses are almost synonymous with deceit? If no one is keeping a score of everything, why bother doing the right things? Why do we feel grateful? Why do we value our own lives? Why do we like and appreciate beauty? Why do we fall in love? Why do we feel grief when our loved ones die? Why does humility exist? Why do we feel compassion for the less fortunate? Why do we celebrate things in our lives? Why is love a universal language?

Which part of the evolution theory can explain all these? It will be hard to find out the exact reason why, solely because we are designed to have meaningful things in our lives. And meaning can only exist if eternity exists, and someone is in control of the eternity. Otherwise, why bother doing anything at all? Everything will be gone when we die. According to the evolution theory, when we die, there is no memory. No emotion. No trace. No soul. No reward and punishment. No heaven and hell. Nothing. We cease to exist. So whatever you did in life is pointless and traceless. Why bother going to work tomorrow? Why bother getting your financial freedom? Why bother even existing?

The point is, nobody likes to be judged harshly. If someone says all the bad things behind your back without even knowing you at all, you wouldn't like it. In the same way, if you reject blindly even the possibility of a Creator, you're not being fair.

I'm not here to convert you to my thinking; I'm sharing with you what successful people do. They think for themselves. They won't reject or accept something until they get to the bottom of it. But this is only possible because they humbly and willingly find out things for themselves. They disregard white noises, they know how to find the truth, and they find them. Look, everyone is naturally a skeptic but it is *impossible* not to know the existence and truth about God if you humble yourself and study the Scriptures in its entirety. Refusing or being willing to study the truth about God can have a significant impact on your holistic wealth because He is unlimitedly wealthy and is the source of any kind of wealth.

Wealth is in abundance and never runs out, but you have to know why. Not wishful thinking but because of the fact that we are anchoring ourselves to the Creator, who indeed has an unlimited wealth. *He is the supreme supplier, the creator and owner of both physical and spiritual world, the time and the eternity, the life and the dead. And that is why God has unlimited wealth. God is wealthy because He gives so much away, and the fact that He gives so much away points to the fact that He is a loving God.* So in terms of physical wealth, any global financial crises or any other crises worries us no more because we are attached to a caring God who has unlimited wealth. But if we think the world is the supplier of our physical wealth, then we would be worried because the physical world has only a very finite supply. And also when we have a firm understanding and belief of God, any kind of loss will not drive us to the brink because we personally know that the real loving God will not test us beyond our capacity to cope.

So worry not about things. What you are worrying about are little things. You should worry about the big things that have far more dire consequences and that are much more likely to affect you. You worry about losing your money, but by not addressing your spiritual wealth, you will lose your life. If you really think about it, no human is really in control. *What can you hold on to in this life? What does the world offer you that is dependable, immortal, and good?* You're not in control of your material wealth; a natural disaster is enough to wipe it all out. You're not controlling your own life, an accident is enough to take it away. So anchor yourself to the God of Divine Providence, who is above all disasters, above all wealth.

But on the same token, just because you will be wealthy when you anchor yourself to God, having lots of money is not necessarily part of the deal. It's a mere bonus. Wealth is not only about money. So it is a heresy and an insult to accuse God of not being able to bless us with such a menial thing out of His eternal wealth and power. Never ever think that if you're lacking in material wealth, you're not being blessed or you are not attached to God. He and He alone has the final say on how to distribute His wealth.

"Where is God today? Why is He not talking to me?" The question should be, why are you not talking to Him? Were you ever willing to hear God, to reach out to His ever welcoming hands? He always reaches out actively, blessing you even when you are unaware of Him or reject Him. It depends entirely on you to reach out to that hand. But how can we even know that? If you are agnostic, then you're absolutely right. There is no way our limited brainpower has the capacity to know whether God exists or not. But the whole game is different from the beginning of time. If you accept your agnostic view, you must also accept that God is willing and has made Himself known.

But which God? There seems to be a smorgasbord of choices these days ranging from money, idols, religion, lucky charms, universe, to ourselves. However, based on analyzes, evidences, and experiences from all major faith systems, the truth belongs to the biblical God. I have never personally seen so many, so good, so real, and so lasting miracles happened compared to other deities. Cancer is gone in the blink of an eye. Terminally ill, near-death patient is healed instantly. The dead is raised a day later. The limp walks. The mute speaks. The blind sees. The broken is fixed. The murderers are turned into saints. Various miracles that nonbelievers can never appreciate and experience. But it is not merely the existence of miracles themselves that is telling the truth, but also the function they serve. When people connect with God, they are finally at peace with God and themselves.

And I'm talking about modern-day evidences. So many of them are reported and documented. And there are so many witnesses, it is impossible to cover or to lie about something so big and universal. Only a wealthy, loving, and real God could have done all these. Most of us wonder what God is like, Him being a spiritual God. So study Jesus Christ, who is God in flesh, whose name is used to perform all those miracles. But again, no one should tell you to believe in God. God doesn't want a blind, robotic faith. He is real, and He wants a real relationship. So as always, research and think for yourself seriously, especially before making an all-important decision like this. You're missing out if you never read the all-time best seller book in the world. Your choice in this matter determines your life and your afterlife.

I hope you can clearly see now that rejecting the spiritual side of wealth will cut you off the branch of the tree of wealth. You're like a light bulb detaching yourself from the wall plug, detaching yourself from the source of wealth. But even more than that, I sincerely hope that you now understand that wealth is indeed unlimited to those who are attaching themselves to the source of all wealth. You can be wealthy even without the possession of physical money. If you are spiritually wealthy, you wouldn't even have to worry about what you will eat, what you will wear, where you will sleep, what will happen tomorrow, and what will happen for eternity. And that is such great news.

Just one more very important thing you have to know in this whole journey of financial freedom. It is fun! On top of some rainy days, your journey will be exciting! Never forget the fun part of this. You'll be experiencing new things. You will meet new and exciting people, go to exciting places. You will be doing exciting stuff. You will be living a life that you were supposed to live. You will be wealthy because your aim is for wealth and life mastery, not money mastery. And now that you have understood the mind-set, you are fit to understand the strategy of financial freedom.

THE STRATEGY OF FINANCIAL FREEDOM

Once you have the right mind-set, you still need financial strategies. Determination alone with the wrong strategy won't work. Persistence using the same strategy over and over again is insanity. Courage with no strategy is blind foolishness. So what we need is well-formulated, concrete, and calculated strategies. The beauty of any strategy is that there is no one perfect strategy. You must be flexible in employing each strategy because each has its own strengths and weaknesses that you must know yourself.

And this is why we need to have the mind-set deeply rooted in our character. Our philosophy, our education, and our character determine our best strategy at all times. Very so until every time we look at opportunities, our brain will automatically think how best to utilize it. We won't be lazy about it, and we will execute all strategies with excellence because we are driven by our wealth mind-set.

You may end up using multiple strategies, but you must first find one and focus, then modify things along the way. Only when one works, can you try another. Not being focused into one is costly. If you are attempting to do three strategies at once, you will violate the mind-set of focus.

In order to formulate your strategy of financial freedom, you must first understand all aspects of it—the what, why, who, where, when, and how.

What Is Financial Freedom?

To put it simply, financial freedom is *a financial state when your multiple passive incomes from your income-producing assets are enough to cover your controlled regular and occasional expenses, leaving you with the freedom of your quality time.*

Let's dissect that definition.

-A financial state. We're focusing on your financial well-being, but you still have to address your interdependence and holistic wealth first. If you don't keep your integrity, if you haven't mastered time, if you don't know what to do when you are facing a setback, you'll never achieve your financial freedom. And being a financial state also means it deals mainly with numbers, strategies, and money. Don't be discouraged. All these are learnable skills.

-Multiple passive incomes. It is an income that you don't have to actively participate to receive. Possible passive-incomes include:

- Positive cash flow from renting out any kind of assets that you own i.e. real estate, storage space, equipment, vehicles, boats, etc
- Positive cash flow from dividend and trading of shares, options, bonds, mutual funds, commodities, or forex
- Positive cash flow from selling the use of intellectual property rights i.e patents, franchises, licenses, copyright, artistic works, etc
- Positive cash flow from commercial business operation or investment
- Positive cash flow from investing or lending your money
- Positive cash flow from ongoing subscription-based service
- Positive cash flow from commission from agency-based service
- Positive cash flow from advertising revenue after you gather an audience
- Positive cash flow from anything else that has common value and stable market

For those who are not familiar with the concept of passive income, think simple. Think of your bank account interest. Once, and only once you've put your money into an interest-earning account, notice two very important things:

1. You don't have to beg your bank manager or do anything for the bank for them to give your interest. You don't even have to consciously remember whether you have or have not received any interest. All you know is the interest is put into your bank account periodically.

2. If you don't touch your money as it grows, the compounding interest takes effect. The interest you've earned is added to the original amount you put in. You're cumulatively earning interest on top of your previous period's interest.

That is basically how people have passive income. Financial freedom is about investing smartly, rarely selling, and never worrying about profit again because you have a passive and constant cash flow. Most people believe more in trading than investing. They are fixated on the idea of buying low, selling high, and getting profit instead of buying good investment, rarely selling, and getting continuous cash flow.

So why don't we just all put our money in the bank? Well, to start with, you have to have a massive amount of deposit for you to earn a significant passive interest, which most of us don't have. Secondly, bank deposit is entirely cash, and cash loses value over time. A $100 note today will buy less in five years' time. Thirdly, if you live by your bank interest, you will have to take out the interest regularly. This loses the powerful effect of compounding interest and that will reduce your financial wealth significantly over time. Fourthly, bank interest rate is within the low spectrum of return rate, sometimes less than the inflation rate. So investing in a bank savings account is counterproductive to financial freedom. Whereas passive income from income-producing assets is on the higher spectrum of return, enabling your investment to support your life. This is then added to the compounding interest and will make it difficult for some people to comprehend how someone's financial wealth can grow so fast.

Notice also when I said multiple passive incomes. It is possible but rare to have just one source of passive income to support your life. It is also risky to have all your effort put into one investment. That is why part of the whole strategy you will learn is to accumulate, duplicate, and diversify your investment.

-Income-producing assets. What is an asset? There are different confusing definitions, but we can simplify it into two. One is the technical or accounting definition. Two is the functional or wealth definition, which is more relevant in real life. Both are applicable for different contexts. The accounting definition simply says that anything you own is your asset and anything you owe is your liability. The wealth definition defines assets as those things that you have control of, not necessarily owned personally, which produce income and increase cash flow. Liabilities are things that you have control of, not necessarily owned personally, which produce expenses and decrease cash flow. To put it simply, cash flow determines if something is a functional asset or a functional liability. With the wealth definition, it is the numbers, not words, that define whether something is an asset or a liability.

Here are examples under this definition:

- Your personal home is a mix of accounting asset and wealth liability. The home is yours legally, and the feeling of owning your own home is invaluable asset, but at the same time, you have to appreciate the fact that your home only incur you expense, no income whatsoever. Therefore, it is a technical asset but a functional liability. Yes, your house has a capital gain potential, but that is not accessible while you are still living in the house.

- Your personal belongings that do not produce income are accounting assets but wealth liabilities. Your car, your clothing, and your gadgets. The point is, it's fine to get all these wealth liabilities, but only when you can afford it. Not when you have to borrow in order to get them. Oftentimes, we jeopardize our financial wealth by giving in to temptation.

- Your business is both an accounting asset and a wealth asset because you own it and it produces income. Once the investment is properly established, your clients will give you profit on top of paying all your expenses related to keeping that business running.

Notice that it isn't just any asset. Your asset must be carefully selected so that they all produce income and increase your cash flow. Owning ten properties all with negative cash flow and capital loss is not going to give you financial freedom. This is why owning an investment without full understanding of it is dangerous at best. So in addition to owning and fully investing in the right investment, you must also understand your investment fully.

-Controlled regular and occasional expenses. This depends entirely on you. *You have to control your expenses, or you will never achieve financial freedom.* It is easy to destroy your creation. If you're greedy or mismanage your financial wealth, then you'll never be financially free. If you earn a million a year from your passive income, you are not financially free if you spend two millions a year or if you keep buying liabilities over your assets. Regular expenses are supposed to be modest monthly expenses that are enough for you to live comfortably. On the other hand, you should never ever scrimp; it's about achieving a healthy balance between your income and expenses. That is why budgeting is important, and you will learn how to do this.

-Quality time. As you should appreciate by now, this is the biggest asset in your life—*quality time in the form of life.* Only when you have quality time can you enjoy and share the good things in life. If you don't manage your time well, you won't get the other things because simply owning a great investment doesn't necessarily mean you will be free. You can work 24-7 in your investment. You can even diversify, but if your business is still dependent on the people instead of on the business system, you're not financially free. You're still trading precious time for money. The aim is for you to trade money with more money.

We achieve financial freedom by having assets large enough to grow by themselves. It's like planting a tree. You water it for years, then one day it doesn't need you to water it anymore. The roots have gone down deep enough, and the tree is tall and leafy enough to provide shade for you.

This summarizes the key understanding in achieving your financial freedom: *Carefully purchase multiple income-producing assets and maximize automation to derive the passive income while living modestly by minimizing liabilities. Then accumulate, duplicate, diversify, and protect your assets until they are large enough to support your life and to grow by themselves.*

Why Do You Need Financial Freedom?

I don't know. It's entirely up to you to know why you want this. It is for no one to influence. Everyone has different reasons. Maybe you want to be responsible to yourself and to your family and friends. Maybe you like to be sure that food is always on the table, the roof is always above your bedroom, and you have the wealth to share all year round. Maybe you don't like the feeling of hanging your life into one job. Maybe you don't like the feeling of relying on everyone else for your life. Maybe you are not comfortable with the idea of working hard all your life while being taxed heavily. Maybe you don't like to have the anxiety about money all your life. Maybe you feel your boundaries in life are defined by money. Maybe you want the freedom more than possessing the money itself. The bottom line is, it is personal, and you alone know why you want this.

In my humble opinion, learning to invest is for everyone, and it is everyone's responsibility. Don't short change your own intelligence and abilities by turning your money over to the experts until you discover what you can do by yourself, which is a lot. And I just think it isn't fair for somebody who knows what to do with your money to use your money for their agenda. If you decide to be ignorant, leave everything to the so-called experts instead of being an expert of your life, then it is really your call. But part of maturing is knowing that you must accept the consequences of your choice.

Who Can Achieve Financial Freedom?

Not everyone. Again, I don't want to give you false hope. Most people are able to do the technical side of investing but most are not willing to invest due solely to their self-limiting beliefs. Like I said, the body is capable, but the mind disagrees. The point is, don't think it's not for you until you try it. It is demanding, it is challenging, but it is fun and very rewarding at the same time.

This is something that has no correlation with age, gender, ethnicity, or background. It has more to do with your view of the future, yourself, and the world. But I also understand that this kind of investing is not for everyone.

For example, if you can climb the corporate ladder, become a high-income earner, and you are happy working nine to five until you retire, then you may not need this. But on the same token, you don't have to leave your job to be financially free. Many people are empowered by the work they do under someone else's business, while being financially free themselves, and that is great.

Where Can You Achieve Financial Freedom?

In most places in the world, wherever you either have access to a capitalistic market or you make such market possible. It is not limited to those countries who openly declare themselves as capitalistic. Even in some non capitalistic countries, some sort of market is possible. It doesn't matter as long as you have your property rights respected by others and by the law, not necessarily formally protected, but at least informally respected. It is less about where you are and more about what you can do wherever you are.

When Can You Achieve Financial Freedom?

It depends on you and your circumstances, your internal and external factors. Everybody is different. No one can or should tell you when. You alone must have the big map and know where you are exactly in your journey. One can achieve it within five years, some less. Some may be longer. But the first few years are the toughest and the time when most people give up. But by now, you should know why you won't give up. Besides, wealth is always around. So the question of when you should start or when you will be free is of less importance compared to when you actually start. People make money on both good and bad times. My advice is to start early; compounding interest is hard to catch up.

The rule is to double your initial estimation. If you have carefully calculated that it might take two years to be financially free, it might turn out to be four years. It is hard, especially when you're not in the power to do things on your own just yet. If it is your first time, you are often dependent on others' action and approval. You wait, and there is little you can do despite diversifying your efforts. And when people say they will get back to you next week, it often turns out to be next month. But it isn't always bad. Sometimes, during my waiting game, I found out things that are not working well. It teaches you patience while opening up opportunities to see things that otherwise remain unchecked.

How Can You Achieve Financial Freedom?

This is where you must understand the technicalities of achieving financial freedom, so we will spend a bit of time here. The application of these strategies will be given in the next part, so focus now on understanding why the following are necessary, one step at a time. Build on from what you already know.

Don't be discouraged at the amount of work you need to do. Even mountains can be moved one scoop at a time. If you diligently do small things, you'll be surprised at how much it adds up over time.

Let's start with the understanding of capital. *You must produce capital.* Capital is value. And people are willing to exchange their money for value. A trip to the supermarket shows that you are willing to give the supermarket some money in exchange of the goods in your trolley because you value those goods. In a capitalistic world, you must be a capitalist and produce capital. *You cannot stay as a consumer and achieve financial freedom. You have to invest in order to give others capital in exchange of their money.* And investing means you have to get something out of your effort, not blindly investing, not leaving your investment to someone else, wash your hands, and expect them to have your best interest at heart.

And value creation means you have to stay original. Emulate others, but never copy. The original always has more value than the copy. And if you don't provide value, you cannot produce capital. And if you don't exchange capital, you cannot have financial freedom. Now, the first thing people often ask is, does this mean we have to get into business? Largely, yes. But it is not limited to traditional commercial business. You can even do things you really love without considering it a business. Better yet, you can delegate the business part to someone else later on. Open your mind first, then make up your own mind.

❖ Start with a journal. And keep it safe.

A journal? Yes, the journey of your financial freedom starts with a humble purchase of a blank book. Never underestimate the humble blank pages. A journal is where you write your plan, your strategies, your success, and your failure. This book is where you will be honest with yourself. You will write your assets, your liabilities, your fears, and your ideas. Don't think all those things are not valuable enough to be documented and to be kept within your reach. If you want to learn from my mistake, buy yourself one very affordable empty book.

But do successful people keep journals? In one way or another, yes. It is impossible to keep track of all the things happening around your investment without some sort of organized way of information system. Maybe you're more sophisticated and use a computer and other gadgets to do it. That's fine as long as you set up an information and archive system that work for you. And keep it safe. Obviously, just as you wouldn't reveal the content of your bank account to anyone, you don't want to reveal your financial situation to just anyone either.

So your first investment is in a blank book. Yes, that is your very first investment, which I'm sure is not as scary as you thought it would be. You will find the cost is dwarfed by the return. This journal will be used specifically for financial information. You'll go back to read it and update it on a regular basis.

Take this point seriously. Without investing in a blank book, this very book you're reading will be useless. Write EVERYTHING related to your financial affairs in your journal and save your brain to think the important things. You'll never know when you will need certain information and how it will save you. Write goals, appointments, discussions during those appointments, failures, what the experts say about your investment, questions and answers, and anything else that needs to be written down. Get a habit of writing things down.

❖ **Create time for you to deal with your financial matters.**

This is when the commitment kicks in. Yes, you work full time. Yes, you're tired when you get home. Yes, you have other commitments to take care of. And yes, there are millions of reasons you can find not to do this. But I used to work nine to five myself. It's more like eight to eight actually, without the overtime pay. It was hard. When I got home, the businesses I needed to contact with were all closed, and they were not open on weekends. And when I seemed to have the time to do things, my friends rang up and told me to attend their events and spend more time with them. I've told you in the very beginning it is not going to be easy.

But you will never have time until you create it. You have to master your time. Part of being financially free is being able to manage your time effectively. Think about it; you have time for those other commitments because you create time for it. Most of us will always create time for meals. Because we think meals are very important investment for us. The same principle can be used here. If you don't think this is important, if you haven't got your purpose rooted on becoming financially free, then you won't find time for it.

I dedicated thirty minutes every day for a start, and I think it's a good start for you too. You must dedicate at least thirty minutes a day to take care of your financial matters, except Sunday. Why not Sunday? *Because too much of a good thing is bad for us.* Either you will get bored, or you will get addicted. You need neither. So the bottom line is, this is just one extra mealtime that I'm sure you can afford. Think of it as you having four meals a day, but the fourth is dedicated to your financial matters. It's hard at first, but most likely you'll spend even more time because you'll be interested at this. Always remember the fun part. This, beyond and above all, is an exciting adventure.

What are you going to do with this thirty minutes? You'll be using this time to read materials, to think, to plan, to call people up, to make deals, to write things down, to invest. You may very well be needing more than thirty minutes because you will be very occupied. You'll be spending most of your time thinking, because the name of the game is to think hard, and less about to work hard, the part which you can delegate to others.

❖ **Start budgeting your way to freedom, now.**

Personal finance doesn't have to be complex, although there are many things you have to consider. *The key is to understand where you are, where you want to go, and how to get there.* Budgeting will take care of the first two, and a plan will take care of the third. Budgeting is about acquiring your financial freedom map and about knowing where you are on that map. It is essentially knowing about what you have, how much you earn, and how much you spend, in addition to knowing how much you need to be financially free and, more importantly, if you started at the wrong place.

The creation, maintenance, and interpretation of financial statements are highly critical in the business world. And they are for individuals too. There are various financial statements, but for an individual, knowing where you are and having a plan to go where you want to go would be sufficient. Different countries have different names for them, but these basic financial statements are commonly called balance sheet, profit and loss statement, cash flow statement, and various other statements. For individuals, let's keep it simple, and combine and call it our budget.

If you don't keep any kind of budget, then start one right now. Use your journal or computer spreadsheet; don't do it in your head. You must write it down, no excuse. There is no right format. Keep it simple. See what works for you. I can only give you simple examples because there is no one-size-fits-all budget. What is essential are the split between assets and liabilities. and between income and expenses. Everybody's categories within these columns are different, so only you know how to separate them. *Understand that your budget is always a work in progress. It never finishes and must be continually updated.* This is where your discipline will reward you. You will always be on top of your financial health, and having this intel is very beneficial in making every of your financial decisions.

First, you need to know your net worth.

Simple formula: Your own net worth is calculated by subtracting all your accounting assets (something you own) with your accounting liabilities (something you owe). This is a snapshot of your financial health. If you already own businesses or companies, include them here. And we want to get periodical personal net worth, so always put a date on it.

Let's start with your accounting assets. Think of all things that you personally own. Then think of its market value today. If you sell all your possessions today, how much cash would you have? That total cash is your asset. No one can get this perfect; the market value of your asset changes constantly.

Just list what you can remember now and keep refining in the future until it is as accurate as possible. If you have an asset with a loan attached to it, don't put the net value of the asset; put the market value of the asset as if it doesn't have any loan attached to it. The loan value will be listed on the liability side. Now think of all your liabilities. Think of what you owe others, any kind of loans: car loan, home loan, personal loan, credit card. If you are to stop and think of all your debts, how much debt in cash would you have in total?

Then work on your net worth, your assets minus your liabilities, to get your equity. Although you can't put it on your budget, your asset includes all your other wealth (health, emotion, relationship, spiritual, time, career), and you cannot put value on all these. So keep in mind that you are starting from the point of being wealthy. This budget only reveals your financial wealth. So even if it doesn't look pretty or you make mistakes along the way, it's not the end of the world. You just have to be responsible for having so much wealth already, then you have every reason to find ways to improve your wealth.

Here's an example of the first part of your budget:

My net worth as of XX/XX/XXXX

Assets value	$ 000s	Liabilities value	$ 000s
Home & content	500	Mortgage	250
Car	30	Car loan	10
Personal belongings	10	Credit card	3
Shares	1	. . .	
Bank interest	1		**B**
. . .			
	A	**Equity**	**A - B**

From the result, you can find out two things:

- If you have negative net worth, don't panic. At least you know now. It is not good to have a negative net worth because some of your income will constantly be feeding your debt. And the larger the negative number is, the harder for you to fix it. Don't worry, it's the start of your freedom. You will be acquiring assets, but you need to reduce your liability along the way too. And as we go along, we will cover a plan on how to reduce your liabilities and increase your assets.

- If you have a positive net worth, then at least you know you have equity of your own. It doesn't necessarily mean you don't have debt. But you're in a better position to start your journey. And some people find comfort in having a massive amount of asset and think that this alone is enough. But even a mountain of asset can be depleted if there is no income and there is no control of expenses. And having a positive net worth has little correlation with your financial freedom. The size of your asset does not indicate the number of hours you still have to put in, in order to maintain your assets.

For you to understand where you need to be, let's compare a financially dependent person's net worth with a financially free person's:

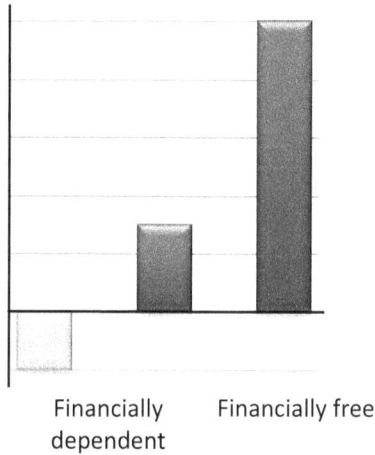

Financially   Financially free
dependent

You'll notice that the financially dependent either has a negative net worth or a little net worth. The financially free has a high net worth due to the accumulation of their income-producing assets. Being financially free doesn't mean that we don't have debt at all. It means your net worth is ever growing.

Second, you have to know your net income.

This is more important than your net worth *because if you take care of your income and expenses, your net worth will take care itself, but the opposite is not always true.* So focus more on your net income than your net worth. Now, you have to know as exact as possible your income and expenses for every month. What you do is to record ALL your regular income and expenses, and yes, I'm talking about including even the small ones because you have to understand that small things do add up, and you have to appreciate every dollar that you earn and spend. You don't have to go to the cents, just round things up. From this you can see exactly where your money came from and went to.

Remember this also. Banks do make mistakes, and unless you do a bank reconciliation, you wouldn't know. A mere look at your statements wouldn't do. You have to actually do it. So in addition to understanding your expenses, you could also be doing your bank reconciliation at the same time. By the end of the month, you should get your monthly income and expenses.

Here's an example of the second part of your budget:

My net income for the month of XX

Income	$
Wages	3000
Bank interest	10
. . .	
	C
Expenses	**$**
Housing	1000
Transport	100
Entertainment	300
Food	550
Clothing	250
Debt	300
. . .	
	D
Net income	**C - D**

From the result, you can find out two things:

- If your income is smaller than your expenses, then that's not good. Again, don't worry. We'll fix it together, but keep in mind that you're endangering yourself of bankruptcy. And the bigger the negative number is, the harder it is for you. Your first priority is to spend less than you earn and to save. Many people fail on expenses. They spend too much. If you can't afford it, then by all means, don't do it and find an alternative. This area is very important because *as long as you cannot control your expenses, you cannot be free.* And this comes back to you personally. You must ask yourself why you are spending more than you can earn, something that is not rational.

If you're in serious bad debt, you must seek help. Financial freedom is much easier to achieve if you begin the journey debt-free, at least with just a mortgage. Bad debt is using the powerful compounding interest *against* you. It's a financial disease. And bad debt is often only the tip of the iceberg. There is a reason behind every bad debt that must be solved first. You must first control your emotion, then you can control your debt. You just have to discipline yourself and get out of debt. Ask for help even from your loan company. Ring them and say you need help to get rid of the loan as soon as possible. Consolidate, refinance for lower interest, and do whatever it takes to get out of debt. Attack the highest rate or the most emotional first. But *never take a loan to cover another loan.*

In the business world, when people start to see continuous negative cash flow, they get really anxious because cash is their lifeblood. A negative cash flow is usually enough to get everyone to take drastic action. The whole purpose of getting into a business it to get a positive income or profit. In the same way, the whole purpose of investing is to get a continuous positive cash flow.

So you must do whatever it takes to make your income larger than your expenses. As we go along, we will cover a plan on how to reduce your expenses and increase your income.

- If your income is larger than your expenses, then at least you're financially secured. You know that by working in your job and assuming nothing out of the ordinary would happen in your life, you can feed yourself and your family and live quite comfortably. But the fact remains, you still have to trade your time and energy to be financially secured. You are not financially free yet, but at least you are financially secured.

Again, for you to understand where you need to be, let's compare first a financially dependent person's income pie with a financially free person's income pie:

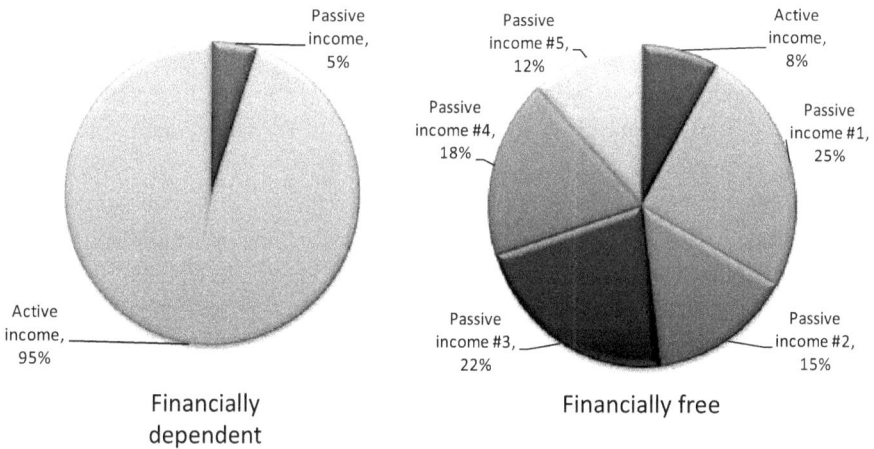

Financially dependent

Financially free

Notice that most of financially dependent people have majority of their income from active income. Meaning, if they don't physically attend and work, they won't get income. This is the case of working employees or business owners who do not automate their businesses. Financially free people have various sources of passive incomes. Each may not be big on its own, but when combined, it will give you a healthy passive income.

You'll notice even the financially free person still has an active income. You still have to work, but you are not bounded by your work. You can choose when to work because your active income will deal mainly with monitoring and maintaining your investments. This is also to prevent you to be complacent and lazy. Besides, working gives you self-respect, self-worth, and dignity, and that is good for our holistic wealth. Any unemployed person would agree.

Now let's look at the expenses. Here's the financially dependent person's expenses pie against the financially free person's expenses pie:

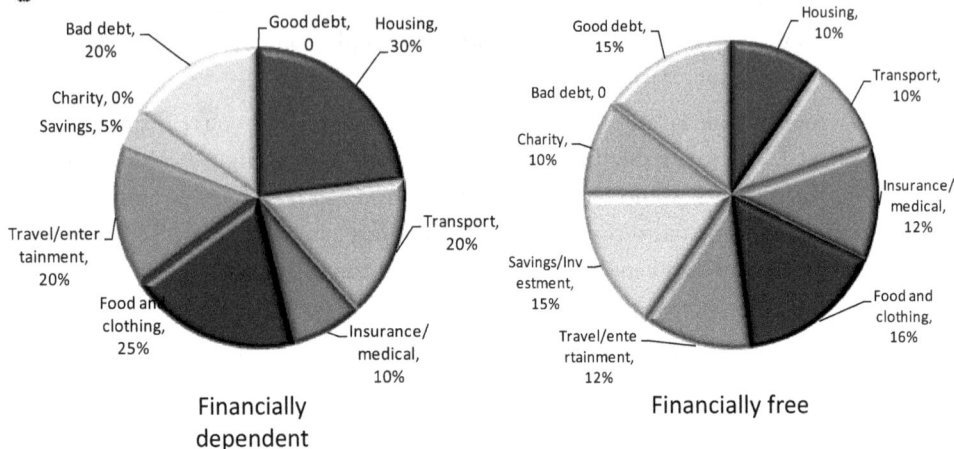

Financially dependent

Bad debt, 20%
Good debt, 0
Housing, 30%
Charity, 0%
Savings, 5%
Transport, 20%
Travel/entertainment, 20%
Food and clothing, 25%
Insurance/medical, 10%

Financially free

Good debt, 15%
Housing, 10%
Bad debt, 0
Transport, 10%
Charity, 10%
Insurance/medical, 12%
Savings/Investment, 15%
Food and clothing, 16%
Travel/entertainment, 12%

Notice that if you add up the financially dependent person's expenses, they total to more than a hundred percent. Meaning, they are living more than they earn. They have a large chunk of their income go to servicing bad debt. And this is not sustainable. The financially free may still have debt. But it is a good debt. They have zero bad debt because they buy all wealth liabilities in cash. We'll talk more about the two kinds of debt and the rule when it comes to getting debt.

☆☆☆

By now you are already taking the first step in taking charge of your finance. You know where you are. You know if there is something wrong and what to address. Let's now set the sail to the place you want to go and learn how to make the plan to get there.

❖ **You must know where to go first, then make and do your plan to get there.**

Having a destination gives you a sense of direction; it tells you what to do, and it provides a path for you to follow. It also gives you control because you know where you are and where you need to go. You are taking charge of what's happening and what will possibly happen. You are in a positive position to reach your destination. In this case, your aim is to gradually increase your passive income until it covers your comfortable expenses. Don't worry, the changes in your life won't be drastic. *You can and should keep your day job as you do this.* Or maybe you have a job that you like, then by all means, stay where you are. Always plan to have fun too. Plan to become a happier person. You have to put fun into your budget and plan. Scrimping is NOT a part of any financial plan.

Begin with the end. List your criteria of success and visualize it first. You must have crystal clear objectives, then work backward. From this list, you can make goals to achieve them. Having a goal makes you a better person already. Think about it. You're no longer like the rest of the population who wanders aimlessly with only a weekend to plan. You're now one step ahead, you are in control. You look at the future with hope, expectation, and excitement instead of fear and anxiety.

Goals also make you more resilient toward short-term setbacks. You will remember the big picture. Your grand design cannot be destroyed by a mere setback. Goal setting is what makes you live differently and getting much more out of your life. Going through life without goals is like blindly toying with life. You are wandering, bumping into things at the mercy of fate. Setting up goals for yourself is much like taking the blindfold off.

Goal setting forces you to first focus your thinking, then your resources, then your actions. Govern the way you *invest*, not merely *spend* your time with goals. Investing means making sure that you will get something out of your investment. There is a rule that if a person invests just one hour a day to study one thing, he or she would be a world-class expert in that subject in less than three years. Big improvements can apparently be achieved with the use of just one hour a day. If you can commit one hour straight at the beginning, then it's great. But it's better to start small; start with just thirty minutes and gradually increase it.

And the beautiful thing about setting goals and achieving them is that at the end of each day, you can see, feel, and know that you have accomplished, learned, and achieved something. You will be experiencing the joy of a productive day. It moves you closer to your goals. It is indeed a good feeling to have used your time wisely and to get something out of your day.

Just a word on goal setting. A lot have been said by many about creating and achieving a goal. Some advocate it; some despise it. But if there is ever a secret, the success of goal setting depends entirely on you. *Do not rely solely on techniques to produce results because techniques rely solely on you to make them work.* So don't question the tools; question the user. Goal setting is one of the strongest tools in the arsenal of success, so use it wisely. And as you have learned by now, when you set goals, your subconscious mind, which is much stronger than your conscious mind, will automatically find ways for you to achieve that goal.

Your subconscious mind is at least ten times stronger than your conscious mind. It is your gold mine for ideas. If you are committed, focused, and positive, your subconscious mind will unexpectedly and automatically give you ideas to solve all your problems. But emotion, visualization, and repeated affirmation are the only language you can communicate with your subconscious mind.

These are the rules of making goals. Very simple, just remember to be SMART.

Specific – You must put a quantity value on your goal. If your goal is to live comfortably, it means nothing. You'll never get that "comfortable" feeling because you don't even know what that feeling is like. Put a dollar value. Look at your budget and determine what your financial goals are.

Measurable – You must be able to see changes along the way. You have to know whether you're going forward or backward in achieving your goals. The result of your effort must be measurable. You must set up an information system where you can see your passive income grows. But it is not limited to income alone. Say you've studied three books, and you have taken out ten main points out of each. That's measurable.

Attainable – Put the word *must* to it to assist your subconscious mind. Plan realistically, so your mind knows for certain that it is attainable. Again, if your goals are humble and realistic, they are absolutely attainable.

Realistic – Don't aim too high or too low. Too high and you won't even be motivated to move off your chair, too low and you won't even be excited to move off your chair. The key is enthusiasm. When you look at it, you must instantly think, "Yes, I can do it. I'm excited by it. And I'm going to make it." Otherwise, your subconscious mind won't believe you and won't do the work for you.

Time limit – Start with long-range to medium-range, then short-range goals and stick with it. You must empower yourself and give yourself a time limit. Otherwise, you will be lazy and complacent. Start with the long-term and sculpt your way down to the shortest. You must make daily goals to do before you start your day. Keep in mind that you're more likely to underestimate than overestimate, so always add a buffer time, but don't use it as an excuse to procrastinate. Time limit creates urgency just like your project deadline in your job. And just like the projects in your job, they get done. Regardless of whether the deadline is real or not.

You must define wealth for yourself, not based on others.

Define the game in a winnable way. Define first your passive financial security number realistically—the amount of money that is enough to cover basic needs passively. Then define specific passive income you need realistically on top of that. Don't aim for both too high. If you can only define that you're financially wealthy when you have millions of dollars, then you'll have a hard time achieving it. If you define your financial wealth to have a passive income twice your rational financial security number, then it's definitely doable.

Think and reflect honestly of what you want. Think of your values, your own real dream, not what everyone else wants you to do. But the more selfish your goals are, the harder for you to get it. The more selfless your goals are, the quicker and easier for you to get it. It doesn't mean you have to start a charity. It means you're doing something with the intended purpose to create value in someone else's life. Write it down. Write the reason why. Write the price you're willing to pay for it. Write how others will benefit by doing it. Remind yourself of these goals. Writing it down is the first step, then the continual reminder feeds your mind with your goals and lets the subconscious mind take its course. Your subconscious mind will work tirelessly until you unexpectedly have a light bulb moment.

Have a list of goals to address every aspect of your wealth.

This is the time for you to sit down and address all the seven types of wealth. Think of what you need to do to address all of them. Think of how to address everything that doesn't work in your life. The scope of this book is to focus on your financial wealth. But you have to prioritize. If you think your first priority is health, then address your health first.

Focus on one goal each time.

Now that you have a list of all your goals in life, the key thing to do is to prioritize and focus on only one goal at a time. The power of focus is the key that unlocks the door to your goal. Goal setting works only if you are focused. When you direct all your energy on achieving a very specific goal, you benefit from the power of focus. *Focus achieves goals.* Here's a little secret to keep you focused on one goal. Each night, write down the ten most important things you want to get done the next day in the order of importance relative to your goals. Then force yourself to get number one done before moving on to number two.

And when you've achieved one goal, you'll be motivated to achieve more. Celebrate then move to the next one. When it comes to celebrating, don't buy or invest on the reward and use it as incentive. You'll more likely to take the reward without achieving the goal. Think of rewarding only when you've achieved the goal. Do think about the fact that you will be rewarded but never do more than that. Focus on achieving the goal, achieve the goal, then think of how you can reward yourself.

Now that you know what your goals are, let's make a plan to get there.

"Failing to plan is planning to fail" as the old saying goes. Having a thorough, working plan is the first and absolute step you have to take. And when it comes to financial freedom, your plan can be reduced to three things:

- The first is to fix what is currently not working and making sure you're ready to invest financially.

- The second is to make sure that you play it safe. Build and don't lose critical money, and protect your investment from possible losses.

- The third is to invest and to nurture your cash flow until it is enough to cover your comfortable expenses, allowing you to be financially free.

So that is how the rest of the book will be laid out. Creating a strategic personal finance plan is enough to cover all these three. You'll start with an empty plan, but as you go through things in this book, you'll end up with something. I want you to produce your own personal finance plan and to be empowered to act it to the end. And as a bonus, some of the parts can also be converted to business plan down the track if you happen to need one to get someone else to work with you.

Here's an example of making a concrete plan and goal-setting.

Plan Making and Goal Setting

In this case, your long-term goal is to be financially free. Meaning, you write it as "In five years' time, by January 20XX, I must have a total passive income of $X per year, which will be enough to cover all my regular expenses of $X per year. Medium-term goal is, in a year's time, so by July 20XX, I must have read X number of books, attended X number of classes on the topic of (your investment), get help to implement what I know from all those information, and I must also have acquired my first investment in (your choice). A short-term goal is, within six months' time, I must have addressed (everything) in my budget that doesn't work. A weekly goal is to start searching the Internet on the topic of (your investment) on what needs to be done. I must have purchased and studied at least five books on it. I must have found out ways to fix things in my budget. A daily goal is to really and actually do this kind of goal setting and plan making for myself."

Think about this: you don't know anything about investment, but you're aiming and focusing to be financially free. Notice the focus; you may have other goals, but you focus on one thing at a time. So what you do is to prioritize; you aggressively seek the knowledge of investment. You set aside thirty minutes a day for the sole purpose of getting closer to your goals. You buy books on investment; you attend seminars or hire a mentor.

By the end of the first month, you'll know what you need to know. You'll probably have read two books on your investment. By the end of the sixth month, you'd have known techniques specific to your investment and how to apply it. You maybe then are confident to start practice or do paper trading. By the end of the year, you're no longer a newbie but an investor.

You would have network with other investors; you would have asked for assistance; you would have started to invest. By the end of the second year, your investment will already be running. You will be automating your investment, getting closer to be financially free. But notice one thing—it comes back to you. There is no point having a perfect plan and goal if you don't do it, and do it to completion. *You must have that love for the game.*

Remember to always write everything down. The budget, the plan, and the goals. And now that you have these plans and goals, let's turn them into a reality by acting your plan. And the first thing to do is that *you must spend less than you earn in order to get the resources to invest.*

❖ Spend less than you earn and always pay yourself first.

You need resources to do your plan, especially for those of us who start this journey with a negative net income. You're in a disadvantaged position if you invest while you're in bad financial position. So accumulating resource to begin with is a must. The only way to do that is to *spend less than you earn.* I don't claim to understand your exact situation, but based on experience in helping others, I found that there are always ways to reduce your expenses rationally so that it is less than your income. Yes, it is not easy or comfortable. And yes, there are financial mistakes that are hard to reverse. But if you are committed, there are ways to do at least to improve things. Look at your budget for a start. See which category of expense is significantly larger than the rest. Think of ways on how you can reduce each expense category. Do whatever it takes for you to have control of your expenses because once you spend less than you earn, there is a space for saving. Saving, at this stage only, is very critical. Saving at the later stage is only done for the liquidity purpose because the rest of your money will be in your investments. Don't save, invest. *Investing is the best saving account.*

"Pay yourself first" is a savings concept you must remember always and apply with discipline. This is the only way to start the path to your financial freedom. It is an automatic savings every time you earn money before you use it. Regular savings leave a leftover to be saved and will give you excuse not to stick to your plan. But paying yourself first forces you to automatically save. You must make this habit. You may think that when you have money in your bank, it's automatically yours. Well, you still have to pay bills and other things, so it really isn't yours until you put it aside as yours. So make sure you really pay yourself first something you really own and nobody else can touch.

Start by picking and sticking to a specific percentage of income to pay yourself periodically no matter what. 10% is the minimum, but the bigger the percentage, the quicker your journey will be.

Now use pure discipline to save 10% of any of your income before paying other things, and never touch it unless you are in a dire financial hardship. On general occasion however, this money is yours and untouchable. No miracles here, just a regular savings strategy and the use of the power of compounding returns. Of course, you don't want to overdo it. You are asking for trouble if you keep 50% of your income early on when you cannot afford it and insist that that money is untouchable. But if there is a leftover, by all means, put it on top of your percentage. Start small and adjust along the way, so you won't feel the difference. Stick to a percentage; maybe you want to increase it, but never reduce it. If you lower it and find an excuse that you need that money for something, that's where the risk comes in.

This is a good time to introduce you to asset allocation strategy. Asset allocation is where you divide your money and decide which goes where. It is a complex business strategy, but in the context of personal finance, it is simply about creating two accounts on top of your daily transaction account:

1. Security account. This is where your "pay yourself first" money goes to. This is an investment in your security. And this is how you play it safely by having a backup first whereas most people invest in risky assets first. Security account must not be touched unless you are under real financial distress. And that's the whole purpose of it—to protect you by having a liquid asset. In this account, *you must have at least seven months' worth of regular expenses.* Why seven months? It is about the real equivalent of six months' real expenses. Don't kid yourself. Despite human's best effort, we still may fail in everything we do. So the sole purpose of this account is to create your financial security for roughly six months, which would be comfortable enough to mitigate your mistakes or for you to start out fresh. And once filled by seven months' worth of expenses, you don't have to worry about it and let the compound growth take its place. You will be surprised at how much it will accumulate over time. Also by doing this, you will only be using the investment money you can afford to lose in case you do lose it. This is the reason why some people lose everything. They start investing before they are financially secured.

2. Investment account. This is where your "pay yourself first" money goes next once you have filled your security account with seven months' worth of expenses. Don't be tempted to take a shortcut. History is filled with people who were not financially secured yet gambled their whole lives on an investment. That is very risky. So make sure the security account is indeed filled with seven months' worth of expenses. Only then can you afford to invest. The sole purpose of this account is to provide you with initial and ongoing capital of your investment. So you should never stop filling it. But the interesting thing is, this account will fill itself up once you are financially free. Your passive and disposable income will be coming from this account.

Some of you may argue that isn't having an income protection insurance what this is all about? Why bother saving up seven months of expenses if your income protection will pay you even more than that? Well, think about it. The insurance will only pay out your claim if you are really incapacitated to work. Do you think you are in the position to invest if you're in the hospital recovering from your injury while still having to deal with insurance claim? Mind you, insurance companies don't just give out money easily. Everyone who has gone through insurance claim will be able to tell you how time wasting and frustrating it is. Look, it doesn't mean insurance is out of question. As a matter of fact, it is necessary in the right situations. We will talk more when we cover insurance.

Some of you may also argue that isn't this security account what retirement savings is all about? Shouldn't we just invest all our money now and let our retirement account take care of our savings? Again, to me it sounds like a herd mentality advice, unless you really know why your retirement account is good for you. How do you know it will be enough to protect you if you lose all your money now? How do you even know for certain that it will indeed grow to your retirement requirement? Do you even know how much exactly you will need in your retirement? Wouldn't it be much better to work hard now to ensure your financial freedom, therefore ensuring your comfortable retirement yourself?

If you've made a careful calculation of your life expectancy and future expenses and you are absolutely certain that saving an $X amount per week now will satisfy that, then the decision is yours. Otherwise, only use it as a backup. It is better to take control of your finances now rather than hoping somewhere along the future you would have enough money for your retirement. Why delay things? My advice is that if you know how to invest your money better now, you should invest it now rather than putting it in your retirement account. It is better to take control and provide yourself and ensure the retirement yourself instead of relying on other people.

Remember that you can only invest when you can afford it. Don't push it, don't rush it, don't get overly stressed about it.

❖ You need to give first before you receive.

If you still don't understand or believe the need to share what you have now in order to get more of what you share, re-read the first section. This is an absolute must. Throw away the idea that you can get a hundred percent of all your income for yourself for the rest of your life and be happy about it. Throw away the lie that selfishness is good for you. Throw away the false idea that keeping to yourself what is entrusted to you for the benefit of others is good for you. *The meaning and the greater meaning of life can only be found in helping others.*

The thing is, giving will always get you back more than what you put in. And that's how you can be happy financially free. It's coming from the spiritual level, and it will give you physical and spiritual returns. Logically, giving is only possible if you're wealthy. What can you possibly give if you are poor?

Giving is about a healthy love of yourself and others. You are becoming an agent of change to make this world a better place. When God gives us 100% and says we can keep 90% but give just 10% He has entrusted to you to help those who need it, He means it. You will love yourself more because you know you are a caring and sharing person. You will be a much happier person because you know you have real life achievements. And when you give, don't worry about what will happen to your gift; it is no longer your concern. Someone may have tricked you into giving them money. Their motive has nothing to do with you. As long as you have done it with a proper motive and in a proper way, surely you will receive your reward.

Start small. Pay yourself first 10%, then give the next 10% out. It doesn't have to be to a formal charity; if your family or friends need your money, give it to them. Motive and action are equally important. You can give with hesitation or with hidden and less-than-noble agenda, but you will not reap the reward. Obviously, we have to use common sense; if by giving it will cause you financial distress, then postpone it. But most of the time, how is that scenario even possible when you're only sharing 10% of what you receive?

You can choose to be greedy and keep everything to yourself and disregard people who help you along the way, but you also have to accept the consequence of accumulating negative energy in your life. There is no other way around it. What goes around must come around. You will reap the good and the bad seeds you have sown sooner or later, in this life or in the afterlife. The scary thing about this is it can usually attack the people or things you love the most. This is not a fear campaign. I don't have an agenda to fulfill if you give money to others. It is a spiritual law. And I would advise that you rather follow this than to make a futile attempt to prove it wrong.

Here's an analogy. A man is carrying $100 with him when he sees a beggar sitting by the curb. Out of compassion, he gives $90 to the beggar. But being a greedy beggar, as soon as the man walks off, he mugs him for the other $10. If you think that beggar is a horrible person, every one of us has been guilty of the same crime. But you may say, "That money is MY money, I worked hard for it MYSELF." Really? Just by yourself? Even a hermit cannot claim that. Did you make the fuel for your car by yourself? Did you plant the wheat for your bread by yourself? Did you create the land your house is standing on? Did you make a conscious effort to make your heart pump your blood all the time? Everything is interdependent, and no one can say they did something by themselves. And just because you paid for things it doesn't mean you can take them for granted.

Every man-made creation, like money, is not designed to last unlike wealth, which was already around even before money was created. And because we're imperfect, our creation is imperfect too. And why are they imperfect? Imperfection means that there is a negative energy attached to it. Money is largely neutral but potentially negative and less positive. The use of money for good intention is dwarfed by evil and selfish purposes.

Giving is about having a powerful partner who could make the entire universe work together with you. This partner is God Himself. In order to receive, you must share. This is the secret. Charity is not just meant to improve the world and those around you. It mostly serves to improve ourselves. Sharing creates room in your life for more blessings to come in. Giving creates an endless circuit. You earn, you give, and then you are able to earn even more.

Tithing is a very powerful way to protect your current and future wealth. In essence, it is an act of purification, cleansing all the negative energy that our money carries. It's removing a small portion of our earnings that represent and will create obstacles and challenges in our lives. Only when we do this will the remaining 90% of our wealth be infused with true blessings, completing the circuit so that we can go out and earn again. Once you begin the cycle of giving, you will not find yourself wasting more money. When you give, it comes back to bless you. And tithing is more than charity. Not only are you making the world a better place, but you're also in the position of bringing justice to the world, making you very spiritually wealthy, and it will snowball to other wealth in your life. You are powering up your soul and paving your road to financial freedom with kindness.

Start sharing as soon as you start to accumulate seven months' worth of expenses in your savings. Now, you need to steer your financial life with prudent financial management rules.

❖ You must practice prudent financial management rules.

This is by no means a complete list of rules for someone to adhere to, but these are essential to make sure your financial health stays healthy. The rest is covered by other parts of the book.

- Every major financial decision must be made based on facts and rational reasoning, not emotion or ignorance. You must gather factual data and think things through and rationally. There is always a way to know more about anything. And the more you know, the less likely you will make bad financial decisions.

- When it comes to debt, there are two kinds of debt. A bad debt is taking a loan to purchase things that will go down in value and will not produce cash flow. It is the power of compounding interest used against you. A good debt is taking a loan to purchase things that will go up in value and will produce cash flow. It's a great leverage to use someone else's money for your agenda. So this is the rule: *Never get into bad debt. And use good debt wisely to achieve your financial freedom. You may only buy things that depreciate in value with cash, never with debt.* You must not buy TVs, cars, equipments with credit. It's a gold mine for the lenders; it's a hellhole for you. Bad debt is bad because you will unconsciously accumulate it and jeopardize your financial stability. Don't think it is natural to have a bad debt. And try to never ever experience bankruptcy. It's about the same as a jail term. It stays forever. Always control spending habits in addition to eliminating bad debt. There is no amount of passive income that will make you financially free if your debt and expenses keep overshadowing your income.

- Never spend more than you can earn. Live within your means. Many people live outside their means with debt. Buy only when you can afford it. Don't involve emotion in your purchases until you can afford to do it. If there are cheaper alternatives, consider buying it until you grow with your wealth. *You must know if it's a want or a need. Buy wants only when you can afford it. Your expenses can only be bigger when your income is bigger.* In every purchase, think of the opportunity cost. Think of what you cannot buy later if you buy it now. *The world encourages you to buy things you don't need. They try to convince you that happiness is in the purchase.* Remember that this is done for their selfish purpose. They try to convince you that you are represented as what you buy, not as who you are.

- I don't particularly encourage the practice of using credit card, unless you have total discipline and know what you're doing. It creates an illusion that you have more money than you actually do. And the credit rating damage is really not worth having. Smart people who use credit cards understand them. If you get it for the rewards program and you have the discipline to pay nothing on your credit card, then it's for you. But again, you can only ride a bull once you tame it. Generally, close the unnecessary ones and use it only for the rewards and emergency needs.

- Do not rely on the social benefit payments. Just as you wouldn't rely on any other insurance payments for your life, don't rely on the social insurance if you happen to be living in countries that do provide them. Consider them as a bonus, but never take them for granted. *Creating wealth for yourself is much more reliable than asking the world for a fairer wealth distribution.*

And just because you pay tax, it doesn't necessarily mean the government has to pay it again to you as benefit payments or pension. They make conscious decision to provide them. So take it as a gesture of good faith, not a silver spoon you are entitled to. And only use it as a last resort. You must be independent. A financially free person never relies on anyone else for income. They take control of their lives.

- No one has the right to dictate you when to purchase your home, when to get married and to whom, when to have kids and by how many, but all these can affect both positively and negatively to your holistic wealth. We will talk more about having a partner and kids later on when we cover your internal team, but for now let's talk about buying a house. Renting is only good for a short term; owning a house will indeed do you a great favor in the long term, but only when it is affordable. Otherwise, it can give you a massive and unnecessary pressure. Buying a home can be a double-edged sword. If your mortgage is more than double of your yearly income, your house is way too expensive for you. *If you already have a mortgage, it might be a good idea to go back to renting and then make your current residential as your first investment property.* If you'd rather stay where you are, then make sure your first passive income is enough to cover the payment. Buying your home with cash may not be for everyone, but buying your home with mortgage when you already have passive income to cover the interest is an achievable ideal.

Now that you have practiced some prudent financial management principles, you should have a bit of savings. So it's time to make your first investment. But before you do that, you must know your financial structure to make your future investment in. It can make or break you.

❖ You must use financial structure to your advantage.

Financial structure is essentially an intermediate between you and your income. The choice is entirely yours, but you have to understand the pros and cons of each before you can make up your mind. Your need for financial structure basically comes down to three factors:

1. **Tax minimization.** *Financial structure is important because it is only the after-tax dollar that counts.* There is no point of earning a large income only to give most of them away as taxes. Having the correct financial structure allows you to enjoy a generally lower tax rate and other benefits accessible only if you are making investment under the name of your entity.

2. **Protection.** *Financial structure is also about protecting your investment and minimizing risk.* A proper financial structure limits your liability in the unfortunate event of you being unable to pay your debt. Your personal assets cannot be otherwise touched by your creditors. But never ever abuse this privilege. It is a financial crime to purposely use a company to get free money. Proper financial structure also protects your assets from certain lawsuits, relationship breakdowns, and unfavorable estate laws.

3. **Control and privacy.** *Having a proper financial structure will allow you to split income and losses and enhance your tax reduction along the way.* You've heard it before—rich people own nothing and control everything. That's because they trade under the name of their companies and, therefore it is also true that under their own personal names, they don't have much. Their financial wealth comes from the companies they control. And you can arrange your structure to provide privacy of your assets, unless you go public.

It may sound confusing for those who never grasp the understanding of creating a company or a trust. Think of it simply as separating your personal need and your business need. Financial structure is about getting a vehicle for the sole purpose of serving your financial needs. Now that you start investing, it is prudent that you have means to focus on your investment in order to maximize your tax deductions, protect your assets, and control your income to best suit your situation.

Your financial structure comes down to either trading under your own personal name or trading using a separate entity that you own. Sole trader and partnership are examples of trading under your own personal name. Company and trust are examples of trading under a separate entity that you own. But you are very most likely need to have a proper financial structure with separate entities to be financially free.

Sole trader – If you are trading under your name, you would have all income for yourself. It is relatively easier to set up, to run, and to dissolve because there are less legal requirements. You would also have total privacy outside the tax office. The downside of trading under your own name is that you will have unlimited liability, meaning if you are unable to pay your debts, your creditors will take your last cent and possibly put you in jail. It is also harder to raise finance. And you cannot split your income and your loss to minimize tax. And very often you will be taxed hardest when you hit a certain threshold limit.

Partnership – If you are trading under a partnership name, it would be very similar to trading under your own name, with the exception being there are more than one of you now. Unless specified, there is a 50/50 split in everything you all do both profit- and liability-wise. If you decide to start a partnership, make sure you are compatible on the personal level. Don't let business experience or credentials alone influence you to take in new partners.

Company – A company enjoys a limited liability status. It has a continuous life. This is why companies can run for more than a hundred years. Owning a company also frees you from a capital gain event in the case of change in ownership in a country that has capital gain tax. If you have an asset under your personal name and you would give it to your children, it would be considered as a transaction or a capital gain event and will possibly attract tax liability. Whereas if you have the assets under your company name, you can just easily change the director name without touching the assets. The downside of having a company is that it is relatively more expensive and more complicated to set up, to operate, and to dissolve. And in some limited cases, a company may not enjoy certain taxation advantage available only to sole traders and partnership.

Trust – A trust is about as similar as it is different from a company. A trust appoints someone as trustee to control the use of assets, and the trust is created solely for the benefit of beneficiaries. They often have different tax and legal laws than a company. You cannot compare them because they perform somewhat different functions and give different benefits. A proper financial structure usually combines them both.

Don't be discouraged by the complexity of your financial structure. A good accountant will be able to set it up for you and explain it along the way. Generally, however, it is almost always beneficial to run an investment on your entity's name rather than your own personal name. Or you may start with your own personal name then convert your business into a company when feasible.

I want to make this clear now. The details of various financial structures are complex. Each person is different, and each country has different laws on financial structures, so you cannot say a particular financial structure is the best for everyone. You must always consult your accountant, tax agent, or lawyer to create a structure that is tailored to best serve your needs. And this must be done early; it will be costly to change things in the future. It doesn't mean you have to create your company today, unless your accountant tells you so. The point of going to see your accountant early is for you to know what exact steps to do once you are ready to invest. And don't be surprised if your accountant says you need two companies for a specific purpose; if they can tell you plainly the need for such thing and you fully understand the benefit, then it's your decision.

Indeed, your adviser must explain to you fully until you understand what they are trying to offer you. But my emphasis on you knowing the basics yourself is that if you know what you're doing first, it will be harder for people to trick you or for you to pay too much. Regardless of the information, they will charge you even for things that are available in public domain because they see it as a form of service. So if you come to them knowing what you already know and what else you need to know from them, you're doing yourself a favor, and you are in a much better position to deal with them.

Now that you know what financial structure you'll need, it's time to do your first investment.

❖ Invest your way to financial freedom.

Investment is a business, and your business must be in making good investments. Most people fail to see and treat it that way. It all comes down to having legitimate businesses and making money work for you. If you're in property, your business can be trading real estate or providing accommodation. If you're in shares, your business can be trading insurances in the form of derivatives or trading ownership of companies. If you are a recording artist, your business is in providing entertainment. The point is, everything you do related to your investment is business, and you must deal with it with a business sense.

You may not realize it, but even a savings account or a managed fund is a business of investing your money in order to get a return. You wouldn't buy a café and let it be run by complete strangers, yet we would invest in a fund that we have almost no control of whatsoever. Your investment must be in your complete control. You don't have to do everything by yourself, but you must set up a system on your investment that helps you in gathering intel, make decisions, delegating tasks, and automating your investment. We'll talk more about business system later.

Before you start your investment, you have to choose your choice of investment. There are only four major asset classes with endless variations among them. And all these share things in common. Every one of them is as risky as anything in life. If they are totally safe, wouldn't everyone be investing in all of them by now? Don't question the risk; question how you can reduce your risk. But whatever you choose to start with, remember that it cannot be just any investment. Any business wouldn't set you free. Your investment must follow these strict requirements to maximize your chance of earning a passive income:

- **The product or service has to satisfy demand both in good and bad economic times.** The purpose of your investment must be to satisfy a confirmed market demand. The nature of your investment must allow it to satisfy that demand regardless of the economic times. For example, during bad economic times, people still need roof above their heads, so certain rental properties will qualify. People still need food for survival, so certain affordable restaurants will qualify. People still need good information to assist them during bad economic times, so certain information product will qualify. People still trade shares. So think of things people constantly need. Look at your own budget; find out what things you purchase all year round. Don't worry about competition. Your business aim is to be unique and excellent. And there are always people who want excellent businesses.

- **The creation of the product or service has to be automatable without your presence.** You must handle the core elements of your investment but the rest must be teachable and support automation. For example, you must know how to set up a burger restaurant yourself but you must also be able to teach someone how to make a burger and set up a system where your system is supervising and employing people to keep making burgers for your customers, so you don't have to be physically there to get your restaurant running and giving you passive income. You work hard once to set up the system, but the system will then do the hard work for you continuously.

  In a similar way, if you have licensable artistic work, your skills are not transferable, but you need a system to market your work. Never ever think that if you are a recording artist, author, inventor, filmmaker, or programmer, then you can just focus on your work and never to worry about the business side of it. Yes, you can hire producers, managers, or agents to help you. But this is one of the most common mistakes artistic people do. *At the end of the day, your work is to make a business out of your artistic work.* If you invent something, don't expect strangers to run your business, and to keep sharing your profit without your participation. The bottom line is, if you want your artistic work to produce a passive income, you must make a business system out of your artistic work.

  On a similar topic, unlicensable artistic work like painting, sculpting, photography, and screenwriting can be a good investment, but it is not a good investment for financial freedom. If you are good at producing excellent paintings, masterpiece sculptures, award-winning photographs, or blockbuster screenplays, your works are very often purchased and not licensable. You'll make significant capital gain but no cash flow. And you cannot teach others to do you what you do and therefore, your investment cannot be automated.

- **The product or service has to be internally expandable without your presence.** The nature of the business must be able to support the system you will create so that your business is able to accommodate extra customers without you putting the extra hours. Going back to the burger restaurant, your system must be able to accommodate high or low unexpected clients without you having to change anything. Your manager may decide to hire or fire staff automatically. That means your system is internally expandable. But externally, in terms of opening branches or making franchises, you have to be fully involved. You want to be involved.

- **The foundation of your investment must be on building and maintaining strong customer relationship and creating a large database of them.** This is very important during good times, even more so during bad times. This is totally within your control. If you are committed to building strong relationships with all your customers, they will trust you for value and will not let competitors sway them based on price alone. If you are only focused on one sale, even satisfying all previous three requirements will not be enough. You must plan to dominate your market on the strong basis of service so that you are subconsciously number one on your customers' minds. Of course, you may need to do certain adjustments during bad times, but your business has to keep all the incentives for your customers to keep supporting you during bad times. The other thing to keep in mind is to go direct to your customers as close as possible, the less intermediaries between you and your customers, the better.

***

Here are four of the most common investments and the broad overview of each. *Remember that you almost always have to acquire multiple amounts within each asset and, eventually, among all different types of assets.*

Real Estate

This is a business of renting, renovating, buying, and selling real estate. It can be residential, commercial, or industrial. Specific to financial freedom, you will mainly be acquiring and holding investment properties. From time to time, you may need to renovate them to increase their value and, therefore, their rents. You may need to sell some when you have too much debt. You will be dealing mainly with agents, bankers, government agencies, and possibly, builders and renovators.

I would strongly suggest that you have an agent to deal with your investment properties. They do most of the automation and maintenance. And the agent fees are relatively lower compared to what they can save you in terms of possible and frustrating headaches. You really don't want to be called in the middle of the night for menial things your tenants are not happy about.

Your passive income will come from the rents your tenants are paying you periodically. Your typical day will include researching properties, visiting open houses, and dealing with tradesmen, property agents, settlement agents, bank managers, government workers, and directly or indirectly, your tenants.

You must own multiple properties to be financially free from investment properties. The rent from one tenant is unlikely to cover all your expenses. Do it slowly but constantly. Be always aware of your financial map, and when you can afford it, always buy your next property. Once you can see in your financial map that you have too much of good debt, then it's about time to sell one of them to repay your loan. At the end of the day, you must study as much as you can about your investment. I think people are attracted to it because it is relatively safer if you know what you're doing. It is tangible, and historically, all financially free people either focus on properties or put their excess money from their other investments in properties.

Shares

This is a business of "renting," buying, and selling ownership of a company or commodities like gold and silver. It can be the book value of the shares/commodities or the derivate value of those shares/commodities. Don't be discouraged by the complexity. It is not easy, but definitely doable. The learning curve is a bit high; the information available to you can be overwhelming, but once you understand the big picture, it is possible to make a constant income out of this investment.

There is a real risk in investing in shares largely because the return depends heavily on future outcomes which are largely vary and unpredictable compared to any other asset classes. But on the other hand, there are strategies you can use on both bearish and bullish markets, as well as delta neutral strategies to anticipate both. Throw away the idea that experts get it 100% every time. They lose money, but their system/software protects them from a massive loss. You will be dealing mainly with brokers, software providers, and possibly, the owners of companies you have a share in. Having an accurate intel and being able to respond quickly to it is essential. Your typical day includes researching the market and the companies, monitoring performances, analyzing share movements, reading the company's financial reports, reading specific financial papers, talking to your brokers, and doing the trades yourself. Your passive income will come from dividends, or derivative premiums, or both.

Cash or Fixed Interest

This is a business of renting your money to someone else to make a gain out of your money then give some of the profit back to you. Bank savings account, retirement account, and managed fund are some of the examples.

It is your share from the profit they made investing your money in something they want to invest in. They are basically intermediaries between the investment and the investor. You have the least control, and therefore, these are relatively riskier. You can research the exact companies these managed funds are invested in, but there is little control except for switching between premade strategies or taking your money out altogether if you know of an impending danger.

Mind you, these managed funds have fees for everything you do with your money—when you put it in, while you're money is in it, and when you take it out. You may only consider investing in a managed fund or leaving it in your interest earning account if you absolutely have no idea of how to make your own investment. The only other reason you want to invest in cash or fixed interest investment is solely due to their liquidity. If you are hooked by the promise of a million dollars in fifty years' time, know that fees and inflation will reduce that significantly when you do have it. You won't do much in your typical day except for researching the best mutual fund, retirement account, or bank account to invest in. Your passive income will come from the interest and share of profit.

Commercial Business

This could be anything. You could be dealing with anyone. This is endless. You can make a business out of anything as long as there is a legitimate market for it offline or online, day or night, local or international, urban or rural, retail or wholesale, independent or multi-level marketing, manufacturing or service provider. You can even invest in people. You can choose to be an entrepreneur or invest in a good one. Nevertheless, you will need to know how to run a business regardless of your choice of business. Core business skills are transferable. I cannot tell how your typical day will be except that you will be dealing with lots of people, doing lots of research, and doing lots of things by yourself. Your passive income will come from the business profit. Commercial business has relatively more work to do but at the same time has the biggest potential for unlimited growth compared to any other asset classes.

If you are an artist, this is a business of licensing your artistic work. And the business side will either make you or break you. You will be dealing with other artists and non-artistic people, who may not understand your artistic vision. Your typical day is practicing, socializing, and working for long hours. Your passive income comes from your royalties, and possibly appearance fees.

In terms of licensable artistic work, you must know that in order to get a passive income out of this, you have to be a solid professional and are somewhere near the top of your field. But there is no way you can know that without trying the market. Artistic industry has the largest amount of disappointed people and the widest gap of income inequality.

Either you get paid lots or nothing at all. And that's where the risk is. But if you have the talent and determination, there is no stopping you. You can only reduce the risk if you are ever pursuing to be the best artist you can be.

Once you have created your artistic work, make sure you protect them. But never ever haste an artistic work because, from experience, it will only become a waste. Get good producers, managers, or agents to sort out your non-artistic matters, but never rely 100% on them. When you are starting out, try to do short or small version of your art. Make short films. Write short stories or articles. Sell mini games. Play gigs at restaurants and clubs. Then move on to getting a demo, getting your first feature film, getting a book publishing deal, selling your programs in the big market.

***

Regardless of your choice of investment, you must be passionate about it and equally passionate about business. Business management is separate to your investment but deserves equal passion from you. Most people go into business with the wrong reason. They pick an emotional reason over the rational one. They passionately love their investments but neglect the business side of it. Not everyone can run a surviving business, let alone a successful one. So if you go to cake-making business because you have talent in making cakes alone or you previously work in a cake shop, then your business won't survive. Because in addition to all that, you have to know how to run a successful cake shop. And the more passionate you are about business, the better your investment will be because they are two sides of a coin.

And remember that talent alone isn't much without passion. Your gift of talent is of no use if your soul doesn't empower it because passion lends itself to hard work. Plus, it will reduce your risk because you want to protect things that you are passionate about. Just on that note, understand that everyone has a God-given talent, but each of us has to discover it ourselves. Never ever say that we have no talent at all. On the same token, never boast your talent either. All of us did absolutely nothing to get any of our talents in the first place.

There's really no point in investing in shares if you don't like it at all. There's really no point in investing in property if you hate property. You won't even be motivated to learn about it. But if you say you don't like to invest in anything, the question goes back to you. If you don't want to do things that may not please you now but will pay off big later, then it comes back to you. This is where you will be confronted with your own choice. There is no way you can achieve freedom without investment. No free lunch. No shortcut. No silver spoon. Never think that the journey those financially free people endured was entirely enjoyable. They were most likely confronted to do things they didn't like, to meet people they didn't necessarily like, or to be in the situation they didn't want to be in.

Going back to the topic of investment, you now have to do a general research on your choice of investment. Try to at least have a broad look at all asset classes before deciding into one. You may like all of them, but you must start with one and focus on only one for now. Only once you've established yourself in one of the asset classes may you diversify.

People often wonder what will happen if this turns out to be different from what they thought it would be. They are concerned with the possibility of changing their mind and preferring something else in the middle of the way. And I did say knowing is not the same as experiencing. That's fine. That's part of your education. However, I would recommend that you make a solid choice based on solid research so you'll be happy to keep focusing on it for a while. But if you're absolutely dreadful about your investment, then change it. Don't linger on it. That decision will be costly, mind you, so make sure you don't waste what you've built so far. Keep it safe. You may change your mind again or need it in the future.

So I hope by now you have picked your choice of investment. Maybe you want to start a café, an online bookshop/e-book seller, a renovating business, a book, a video game, a music CD, and the list goes on. Regardless of your choice, education must be your first real investment.

❖ Your first real investment must be in your education. Full stop.

The best investment ever is your education. You buy it once and use it forever; giving you return over and over again. *Once you put your money in your brain, no one can take it away.* This alone guarantees your financial freedom. This is the template you can use regardless of where your starting point is. As you would know by now, it is not necessarily about formal education, but never disregard formal education either. Formal education greatly advances people's lives, the community, the country, and the whole world. Think how important formal education is to all the doctors, lawyers, accountants, engineers, scientists, artist, and others. I'm only saying that I have yet to find a formal course that teaches people to be financially independent. So use any information that you can use in order to achieve *your* goals. Your education is what produces *your* result regardless of where it's coming from.

Education gives you a massive leverage. It's about learning from someone's experience, which may have cost you lots otherwise. And you certainly need leverage. If you're already working full-time, you won't be able to do much without leverage. To put it simply, *leverage is the power to do more with less.* For example, getting a good debt to finance your investment is a leverage because with a little money of your own and a lot of others', you are able to purchase an otherwise unattainable investment, and to purchase it for your own benefit.

But leverage is a double-edged sword. It can work both ways. Your losses can be amplified. If you refuse to learn, that ignorance will lead you to even knowing less of what you know. You must be constantly and habitually fed by quality information. And when it comes to reading a book, attending a seminar, buying a program, or hiring a mentor, I don't want you to just listen to them or read them, but study them.

Before you study anything however, you need to know *how* to study. Reading, listening, and remembering alone do not necessarily mean studying. And this often becomes the missing link in our education. *Studying means understanding something fully to a point that you can write the main points and know how you can use it. And then you use it.* Study skills include: How to read quickly and effectively; how to concentrate to absorb information rapidly and comprehensively; how to listen actively; how to organize and remember things accurately; and most importantly, how to spot opportunities to apply what you have learned and how to apply it.

I cannot tell you which is the perfect book, mentor, or program for you because, one, there is no such thing and, two, you'll learn a lot when you receive conflicting ideas from people. No financially free person learns everything from one source. They travel all over places collecting gems of wisdom. So the searching itself is part of your education. You'll learn how to filter the wheat from the weed, the truth from the lies. You'll begin to see which topics and subtopics are important. You'll develop a strong problem-solving skill.

Do a research on the topic of your investment and all the related books, programs, coaches, gurus, etc. See their ranks in major shopping sites. Always check reviews and check the author's credibility. More importantly, see their results. Listen to their valid customers, not the paid or fake ones. Buy five books for a start on the topic of your investment. Buy these books while you're accumulating your seven months' worth of savings. *You must start studying when you're starting to save.* Attend free seminars. Talk to people already in the investment on your choice. Join clubs and networking events specific to your investment. Ask around for reviews, what works, and what doesn't. As always, filter their comments and use good judgment along the way.

You must learn how to gain intel on your investment yourself. Being educated in your choice of investment means you are prepared for anything in your investment. You may have to hire coaches to give a hand-on experience. You may have to purchase relatively expensive programs. Do whatever it takes for you to be good at your investment, as good as you are at your job. I'm sure you don't often make mistakes and you produce consistent results; otherwise, you won't be in that job by now. Regardless of your employment status, *you have to be certain that you know what you're doing because reality validates your education on a constant basis, and it is not very forgiving.*

Your lost money cannot be recovered; it can only be replaced. You will still face failure no matter how well prepared you are. But I just don't want you to be complacent with anything. *Aim for perfection and settle with excellence.*

You have to know your numbers in details. *The main aim of education is to benefit from specialized, focused, and detailed knowledge.* You'll know exactly how to tell a good investment from a bad one because you'll know how to make a thorough calculation of numbers. *The dollar is in the details.* Before you purchase any investment, you have to do the financial calculation so thoroughly that you can accurately predict the cash flow you will get. This is not impossible. It's about getting the big and the small pictures, writing everything down habitually, collecting valuable info accumulatively, putting some contingency money on it, and have a thorough assessment on it. It will come with experience.

And while this side of education is ongoing, you must educate yourself in something else—your current job, if you have one. Why? You may say you already know how to do your job. But the aim here is to learn business skills and systems. It is a great opportunity to study someone else's working business before you start your own. Learn as much as you can from your current role. Write things down. Study why someone needs to do your job description. Think of why you are paid to do the things you do. Study your role, and if possible, study other roles.

Analyze how things work together in order for your organization to run. If it is a small business, ask your boss if you can help or study other roles than your own. If you're in a big business, consider moving between departments. You will learn a lot. Study why particular things need to be done in a particular time. Study their mistakes too. If you don't like your supervisor, ask yourself why, because eventually you will have your own employees, and you better make sure they are happy working for you.

When it comes to the decision of whether you should get a college degree or even get in debt to get a degree, the question goes back to you. Know this—a proper college degree can propel your career if you're thinking of going to work with someone but less if you think you will be working for yourself. A college degree is always a good addition in your education, but when thinking of getting one, you should really ask yourself: Are you going to be fully committed to your study, or are you clueless of the whole point of going to college for the sake of just getting the degree? A half-baked degree plus debt to acquire it can wreak havoc on your financial wealth. Not many employers hire average graduates, let alone less than average graduates. So the bottom line is, get it only if you know exactly what course you want to do, how you will get a job via your degree, and how committed you are and how you can excel in your degree. If you want to study only for personal reasons, wait until you can afford it.

❖ You always have to minimize risk.

Your journey to financial freedom is a holistic one because it is synergistic in nature but often fragile. Just one little thing we don't take care can potentially destroy everything we've built. Investment-wise and noninvestment-wise, risk is always around. *But avoiding risk usually leads to another risk.* The only thing to do about it is to learn how to manage it, and not tolerating it. Most people prefer to be ignorant and expose themselves to risk rather than taking control of it. "When it happens, it happens," they say. But that's not being responsible. Besides, if something bad does happen, it's not going to be pretty, and we don't know how extensive the damage will be.

Investment is about taking a calculated risk that increases the likelihood of the reward. *Risk can be greatly reduced by acquiring and using relevant information. What you know is wealth. What you don't know is risk.* Now, you've heard it before. Risk generally equals return. Higher risk, higher return. But in this case, you must minimize risk and maximize your return. The more you know how you can reduce your risk, the more return you can get. And just on that note, you must avoid gambling altogether or, even worse, getting in debt to gamble. It is silly risk. If you think you're addicted to gambling, you must seek help.

The number one tool to minimize risk is education by yourself. Education alone can tell whether you are buying a good or bad investment, getting the truth or lies, basically separating the right and the good, from the bad and the wrong information. Education alone can objectively assess the risk of an investment and helps to find out ways to minimize it, and to anticipate changes in terms of market, regulation, and technology. And you must do this by yourself. You don't want to delegate the control of risk minimization to anyone else. It doesn't mean you don't need the help of insurance companies or other people you can hire to manage risk, but you have to know why you need it in the first place and how exactly it will reduce your risk.

No doubt, you must seek experts' councils at times, but you must keep learning to be the expert in making your own decision, especially for things like your own marriage, your own kids, your own personal health, your psychology, and your own financial matters. It is dangerous to leave these things for others to decide. If you fail, then at least you fail yourself, and you'll learn very valuable lessons from it. For someone to come to you to offer these decisions, they must have their self-interest. So think for yourself because everybody can be wrong. Don't just give your money away because you don't understand something. Learn to evaluate and make better decisions instead of shortchanging your own intelligence and abilities. Taking control of your money is taking control of your life. No one cares about your financials except yourself.

So come to think about it; education gives you control. And you must retain control. Think of when you travel by car. Imagine you're in a car travelling without the control of a steering wheel, the gas, and the brake pedal. You will be at the mercy of fate. And risk is totally out of your control. But imagine having the convenience of a steering wheel, brake and gas pedal, a GPS system, AND the privilege of having your loved ones in the same car. One, you would feel more comfortable and much more in control, and two, you would try your best to protect your loved ones.

So basically, if you can directly make changes in your investment, you are in control and in a better position to minimize risk. And if you know how this will affect your loved ones, you will pay more attention to reducing risk for them too. *At the end of the day, it's really not about risk tolerance but risk management.* And risk management is an ongoing thing. Meaning, you must keep doing it, reducing risk as you go. Initially, you cannot minimize all risk; you can only keep reducing it along the way. That's why you need to start small.

If you have done things like your budget and your plan, you'll be in control if your family asks for a holiday, new car, new house, and other things. You can then reflect on your budget to decide. If you don't have any control of your money, you might go on impulse and jeopardize their other financial needs. And when you're in control, you'll automatically be happier because you know you are taking an active approach to avoid undesirable things from happening to you and your family.

Specific to financial freedom, here are the most common threats:

Damage to investment. This can range from physical damage to anything, but most likely, there is insurance or some way to protect your investment from it. Prevention is much better than cure, and all damages are related to risk minimization and therefore, control. Intellectual property (IP) protection is a must if your investment involves something original, which may require a patent, copyright, or design protection. From others' experiences and my own, getting a patent does *not* guarantee protection, especially if you are fighting against big companies. Big companies can afford long legal battles, but most of us can't. It does establish you as the original owner of your work, but the only solution to IP protection is to first protect it rationally with patent and copyright, try to have a trade secret and focus on creating the best product you can. *Your point of difference is your best protection.*

Other damages can be more physical like accidents, natural disasters, theft, etc, and that is why proper insurance and proper control related to your specific investment are a must. Insurance is a topic nobody likes but needs. See it as a way to protect your hard work. There is no point of building something up only to lose it accidently because you're not covered.

It is relatively cheap compared to the possible damage you have to personally recover. So find out early, research thoroughly, and don't delay on buying the necessary insurances. Focus on insuring yourself and your family because you all are your biggest asset. Start with health insurance, then proper insurances specific to your investment. Insurance gives you the peace of mind knowing that in case something will go wrong, your loss will be minimized. Think of the possible loss. If you can have peace of mind just by purchasing insurance, think of how much it will save your health. A dollar amount cannot be paid for the health damage that stress and anxiety can cause.

Relationship breakdown. Now, marital relationship is complex, and divorce is a horrible thing for anyone to go through. It is long, painful, and very draining. So the first question people often ask is, should we consider prenuptial agreement? I can say this frankly, *it is better to be a good person and marry a good person and aim for a fulfilling marriage instead of relying on things like a prenuptial agreement.* Even if both of you decided to sign for it, and your marriage end up in divorce and you retain all your money, you would still lose the biggest ally in your journey toward financial freedom. You will not be wealthier just because you didn't lose money in your divorce. As a matter of fact, you will lose a partner, time, energy, and effort dealing with your divorce. That by itself is a lot of loss of wealth. Marriage is not something to be hurried or influenced by none other than you two. *It takes much more than just love for a marriage to survive, but it should be based on the foundation of love.* The priority should be on finding the right partner. And this takes time, energy, and commitment long before marriage. Many people get into marriage so easily and unprepared to accept that their romantic dreams are often unmet in reality.

Taxation. The funny thing is that the government actually rewards those who are trying to make wealth for themselves. You'll notice how you will pay less tax as you make your investment. Now, taxation is complex and can impact your financial wealth significantly both in this life and, believe it or not, in the afterlife too. Dead people still get taxed. So clearly, you have to attend your taxation matter. But taxation strategies are dangerous if not executed with full understanding of the implications. The key is to plan ahead and to have a *good* accountant to help you along the way. How do you find good accountants? Find someone who speaks on your level and can show clearly how the advice can be acted and produce result. Someone who listens. Someone who cares about your taxation affair. Someone whose favorable actions speak louder than his or her favorable words.

Taxation is also directly related to your estate. You must create your will now and take care of how your estate will be distributed in the event of your death. A will is simply a legal document that sets out your instructions for the distribution of your assets and liabilities when you die.

Debts and many other things stay after your death. So be responsible and make it as smooth as possible in case of your death. Specify it in a personal letter. Not having a proper estate planning can significantly impact your wealth and will only benefit the third parties involved. And remember to keep updating it regularly as your circumstances change. The last thing you want is for your estate to go by the estate law set up by the government. Your estate will be taxed heavier, and the distribution may not be how you like it to be.

On top of all that, always be careful of signing anything down. Be aware of the legal consequences in everything you do. Also always be specific when it comes to getting information. If, for example, you ask someone what the differences are between A and B, and they say "about the same," it means nothing in terms of intel. Find out exactly what the similarities and the differences are. It goes back to having education as your best policy. And once you have your education in place, risk is really not an excuse not to do something.

The bottom line is to protect yourself and your family first, then protect your investment as you make them. Once you are protected, you need to upgrade your skills specific to your journey.

❖ Learn all the skills you need on your financial freedom journey.

The following skills are all interdependent but must be independently addressed. All of them are learnable and time-enduring skills that you personally have to learn before possibly delegating them. It may sound much, but small steps are always the key. You have to go through the process yourself. *Research, research, research. Penetrate through the unknown, the lies, and the conflicting ideas with thorough research.* It is part of your education; you cannot skip it, or you will fail. Start small as you perfect one thing at a time. *Everyone is good at things they invest themselves in, and everyone gets better with practice.* And eventually, you'll be an expert yourself. Understand that all financially free people are experts at something, and that's why they thrive regardless of the economic condition. Become a master of where your investment is because skill makes all the difference. Invest in yourself first and be great at something.

In every one of these skills, you need to fully understand what you're doing. We're talking about the need to purchase real education programs, preferably with mentoring, because a little education is dangerous, and small things you don't know do add up. Both of which can threaten your financial wealth. This real education is readily available, but of course, they come at a price. There are always people who are willing to share what works for them in exchange for money. That's fair. And you should know by now that the cost of your education is negligible compared to the benefit, and you won't let your grand design be destroyed by your ignorance.

Investment skill

This is the technical nuts and bolts of your choice of investment. This book covers the strategy and the technicality of financial freedom, but you still have to learn about the technicality of your investment. It is unfair for me to cover just one particular investment skill and not the other skills for those who prefer them. But if I put everything in this book, it will no longer be about financial freedom but about technicality of investments, which is readily available.

And once you have your investment skills, you must find your own investment opportunity. Go direct and buy investment properties, and provide accommodation straight to your end customers. Build an online business, and provide goods and services straight to your end customers. Letting others take care of your investment wouldn't serve your best interest. Create your own investment instead of relying on others to do the hard work for you. Think about this: if one investment is so good, the bank wouldn't lend the money to you; they'll buy it themselves. And that's exactly what's happening right now. Banks buy the best investments for themselves and give the less good ones to you in order for them to make a profit on an otherwise unattractive investment. And we wonder why they make so much profit.

Take things easy. Start small. You don't want to be overwhelmed when you're starting out. Start with paper trading or practice. Do it as if you're doing it for real, but don't use your money on it. You can only use real money when you're totally confident. Draw out exactly what you are thinking of doing and realistically calculate how the market will respond, how the bank will respond, how the cash flow will come in. Practice for the first few months, especially if share trading is your first investment option.

Marketing skill

Marketing skill is quite superior because it connects you with your client. *Without your clients, your business is nothing.* Your business may have the best product or service in the world, the best system, the best suppliers, but if you don't have clients to support your business, you'll be running an empty office. That itself should be enough to humble every business person.

Marketing is problem solving. Marketing is telling people that you are a source of value to better their lives. Marketing is the way to accentuate your unique selling points. Marketing is about making money in ordinary businesses in extraordinary fashion. Not everyone realizes that money is a dead thing that doesn't have conscience and is only attracted to marketing and nothing else. That's the best and the ugliest part of money. Best because it is something everyone can equally learn to get and keep. Regardless of your background. Ugly because it has no morale or integrity attached. Money is not going to stop you if you use it for less-than-noble purposes.

Marketing often has a bad name because people confuse and relate it with sales. *A sale is only a natural progression of marketing, but marketing should never get bypassed.* Often people just want to sell without telling you why you should buy in the first place. They fail to understand that marketing is a relationship. *You must build a client database and stay in touch with your clients.* So your aim is to focus and stay on the marketing side and let sales occur naturally, because selling is a bad image to portray to your customers.

You must be in marketing business regardless of your actual business operation because all businesses are fundamentally the same, superficially different. And marketing links them all together. Learn as much as you can about marketing because *cash flow is determined almost totally by your marketing. Cash flow is the direct result of your marketing.*

Learn to use emotional and value direct-response marketing. It is a necessary evil tool. I advised you not to be emotional in your purchases, but here I am advising you to entice buyers with emotion. I'm not contradicting myself, I'm only sharing what works and value must always be the priority and be above selling because your customers will eventually find out. *So provide value then find out and use the emotional reasons from your marketing research on why your clients should get the value from you, and buy from you now, and buy from you later, again and again.* There are too many bogus, useless, or even damaging information out there, so it is one of your marketing challenges to filter them all and gain your clients' trust to give them a break from all the junk they are bombarded with every day. *Trust is the driving force of business.* It can be sped up, and it is a learnable skill. *The level of trust your clients have on you equals your result. Trust affects everything. Your testimonials will speak for themselves. This is why you must make integrity your cornerstone.* I'm sure you are unlikely to go back to a business that has blatantly or subtly ripped you off. And you just have to accept that even though people may compromise their own integrity, they still expect and demand you and others to have it.

You will also need to learn technology. You cannot lose learning about business and technology. The world has become largely business and technology driven and dependent. You must know how to use technology to complement your marketing. Internet is a must. It is here to stay. It has unimaginable potential to help your investment. *You need to have online presence and online marketing strategy regardless of your investment choice. You must be committed to create a functioning and selling website, or don't bother. Don't think that just because you have a website, your customers will flock to you.* The good thing is you don't have to know all there is to know about the Internet. Besides, you can always hire someone who is good with the Internet. The small details may change on a daily basis, but the functions they serve stay the same, and you must know how these functions serve your investment needs.

Management skill

Whether you are aware of this or not, your journey to financial freedom is a project, and more about the sum of the individual parts of it. It's about managing time, resources, stress etc. It is a coherent project that you must manage simultaneously. You will need to manage people, legalities, systems, decisions, and most importantly, cash flow. And you will need your management skill very early on, because the first few years are the most demanding. And this skill determines your other skills. *How you plan, organize, lead, and control your resources, time, and energy to manage one thing in your life will affect other parts of your wealth.*

Leadership skill

Anyone can be great leaders. Throw away the idea that leaders are only those who lead the nation or big companies. *Leading is simply the art of influencing people to be better.* Great leaders are those who influence people to bring the best out of themselves in a positive way spiritually, intellectually, physically, financially, and relationally. Therefore, you must be trustworthy, filled with integrity, and have a positive vision and outlook in life. In your journey, you will be recruiting and leading people, so this is a critical skill. You are to lead others to help them change their thoughts, beliefs, and actions for the better. This will decide whether people want to work with you or not.

When it comes to hiring people, the question should not be how you can hire the best person to do the job but how you yourself can attract the best people to work for you. If you happen to be lucky and get great employees but you are lacking in leadership skill, sooner or later they will notice it, and they will abandon you. Great people need to be led by great leaders. It's their demand. As you work on your investment, as you grow and learn more, you'll be more attractive in terms of being an employer; and employees will flock to you. If you want to get something done right, don't do it yourself. Be a great leader so you can hire great people who can do better jobs than you, even run the investment for you. Remember also that your employees are your reflections. What they do, both good or bad, are often a test of your leadership skill. So while you have to be good at team building and relationship building, you must also be good at building your reputation.

Communication skill

I cannot stress enough how important this is. Relationships are a wealth-creation tool. If you are not a good conversationalist, a good listener, it will be impossible for you to achieve financial freedom. You need to train yourself to be a better communicator. You cannot be a difficult person. You are judged by what comes out of your mouth—your choice of words, the level and diversity of your vocabulary, and how well organized the thoughts you express are.

Be a good communicator. For good or bad, your conversation is your advertisement. Every time you open your mouth, you let the world look into your mind. So your attitude and personality must not get in the way of your prosperity. You must have good personal image, and your enthusiasm will spread to your customers too.

Building personal and professional relationships are fundamental to your wealth. Financial and communication skills are equally absolutely necessary. Be polite, be courteous, and be pleasant. But at the same time, be firm, be assertive, and be bold to get what you want. By experience, you will often have privilege access you don't otherwise get if you had not built the relationship.

You will be faced with conflicts, externally and internally. Your outer circle may have a conflicting interest with you, and your inner circle may not understand what you're trying to do. *Your communication skills will be tested during conflicts.* And communication is not about verbal alone. Your body language pays an important role too. All these on top of your action. For example, how you express gratitude toward people who have helped you along the way really counts.

And finally, you are never alone; there are many in your journey. So you must network with them. *Your network determines your net worth.* Never underestimate the power of meeting the minds of same interest. It is the power of subtle influence at its best. If you hang around with successful people, their success will be contagious to you. Close associates are usually the first to be offered closed-market opportunities, unavailable to the mass. And history is filled with success stemming from simple networking. But no opportunity will be opened to you even if you are surrounded with the best people if you don't open up and communicate properly with them.

❖ **You need an internal and external team.**

The term self-made millionaire is arrogant, foolish, and untruthful. If someone can climb a mountain by themselves, one thing you can be sure of is that it's not a big mountain. No one in their sane mind could say that they have achieved everything by themselves. Even before we were born, we need nine months of intensive care from our mothers. You will definitely fail if you want to do everything by yourself and refuse the help of others because you will be departing from the point of greed and arrogance, repelling those who can help you out. And that's also the reason why we have to share because in one way or another, people share with us and help us along the way.

Never ever think you can do this by yourself. No one can ever achieve financial freedom without the help of others because financial freedom is a team effort, and therefore, you can never boast your achievement.

Remember that we are the sum of all people we have known in our lives. Having a great team is also a great leverage. You are using other people's time and energy to your advantage.

Internally, your family is your biggest ally. They have to understand and participate in the journey. There must be a covenant to show your commitment to your family and to your future together, and they will have to make the same commitment to you. Start by honestly discussing where you are financially and where you want to go. Discuss and share the budget. Talk about how each of you should give and take for a more prosperous future. Everyone should be on the same page because a family is in the same financial boat. Each person must take personal responsibility of controlling their spending. Promise that each will control their expenses, be charitable, not to hide any debt or secret purchase, and promise to be patient with one another through the transition to a better life. Have a constant reminder for your covenant. It serves as a bond of faith among all the members of your family.

Your partner can make you or break you. If you and your partner are not in the same financial mind frame, your financial endeavors will not be fruitful, and chances are your relationship or marriage won't even work. Financial problems are the number one cause of divorce and can bring out or aggravate other problems. Reaching financial goals always take a little bit of sacrifice, and it would be impossible to do it on your own. Understand that mutual sacrifice is a healthy part of your marriage. Talk this through with your spouse gently and in a non confrontational way and get him or her to support you. *It's not about controlling each other; it's about being honest and caring for each other.*

Externally, you may need business partners. You may need mentors. You may need employees. And you will definitely need experts' councils. You must bounce ideas and get feedbacks, and have someone to professionally validate your idea. You must delegate things you cannot do. You must buy other people's time because you cannot buy more time. Working smart means letting the smart people do the work for you. *Intelligent people hire people who are more intelligent than they are.*

How do we know which things we can do by ourselves or pay someone else to do it? When do I need to delegate? There are certain things that would be much better for you if you seek and pay for professional help. Yes, they are costly, so you have to be sure the service they are providing is absolutely needed. When I created my first invention, being a non technically savvy person, I didn't have a clue what to write in my patent application. When I paid *a lot* for a lawyer to do it and looked at what they did, I realized then that I would never be able to protect myself fully had I done it myself. They described the details and the functions I would never have claimed. But on the second invention, using that as a template, I could fill out the patent application properly myself.

On the other hand, even though people say you should get an accountant to create your company, I found out that I could go directly to the governing body and do it myself. But that's because I knew exactly what I was doing and so I saved heaps. *So the key to when to use someone else's service is to understand the detailed steps you need to take in order to get what you want, and assess whether it is feasible to do any of the steps yourself or hire someone else to do it.* You have to know what the intermediaries are. What really needs to be done? What resources do you have or don't have? Can you do it yourself the second time now that they've shown you how to do it once? Then you can decide.

You must know what you're doing before approaching a professional. You don't come to them and ask what you should do with your money. You must come and say, "Here's what I'm going to do with my money, what do you think? How can you help?" Every professional already have their own network of commission, so they will always suggest something that they have financial interest in. The product they suggested may be great indeed, but make sure you think objectively.

Experts - You need experts on your team. People like accountants, tax agents, and lawyers. You must seek advice on things you're not an expert on. They have been around in business longer than you, and their experience can save lots of trial and error. And pay your advisers well. The power of good advice will outweigh the cost. Always seek their advice *before* you do any investment.

Employees - You must find yourself great employees. And your employees are great because you are great. This is why you need to develop your leadership skill. And I'm not only talking only about the high-end jobs. There are never ever such things as menial roles. Every one of your employees must be given equal respect. Businesses can fall when the menial jobs are not done properly or the people who are doing it are not given their due respect. The bottom line is, staff will make you or break you. They will support your vision or refuse to do it. *Hire carefully, train them heavily, and invest in them always.*

Business partners - You may need to do a joint venture. It is a great and easy way to start a business if you all have complementing skills and resources. But that alone should never influence your decision. Taking cold business partners can be risky. You have to be compatible on the personal and the professional levels. Your life and business culture must be mutually shared.

Business mentors - You may need to hire a business mentor to help you step-by-step. Nothing replaces instant interactivity and instant feedback. Advisers are only there to answer your questions, but good mentors hold your hand in every step of the way. They can be costly, so think carefully. And again, it is almost the same as having a business partner. Make sure you are personally and professionally compatible.

And just like everyone, every mentor has different talents. Some generalist, some specialists. Hire according to your need. And always use good judgment as there are many fraudulent business mentors out there.

You are now much well prepared than most people to start an investment.

❖ You will need the initial capital. Think creatively.

You must only proceed once you have your seven months' worth of savings put away safely in your savings account and there is a surplus on your investment account enough to start your investment based on your thorough calculation, which you should have done by now. Make the best effort to make your first investment with equity only, except if it is a large investment like buying your first investment property or opening up a new restaurant. There are many businesses you can set up with relatively small capital. Setting up an online business, setting up a trading account and making the first few transactions, or writing a book does not cost you a fortune.

You can be creative. Other than using your own money, there are other ways to get finance. But in of all these, you better have *a solid business plan and solid communication skills* beforehand. It would be very hard to convince anyone to invest in you unless they can see that you know what you're doing:

Get a loan and use somebody else's money. In the event that you do need good debt leverage, make sure you can fully benefit and pay back the loan. *Shop around and don't focus on the interest rate alone. Pay a very good attention on the terms attached to the loan.* Good debt is called good debt because of the function of it, not simply because it is buying something that will increase in value in the future. Make sure it serves your purpose, so you have to know the inside out of the loan.

Sell the shares of your investment. You may have little at the beginning, but that's what selling shares is all about—the promise for bigger future returns in exchange of providing you qith the initial capital now. This can be done by approaching the so-called angel investors or venture capitalist. Search offline and online for them. But remember to protect yourself and your investment. There are many fraudulent people who see you as a gold mine of ideas to steal from. And if you do proceed, make sure you connect on personal and professional levels. *Make sure you fully understand the terms and conditions of their finance because they usually want a voice in how you run your investment.* And always set the rules in stone with or without the help of a lawyer.

Ask from anyone you know. Family, friends, or even random strangers. Your inner circles are usually easy targets. Depending on your family, you can usually get a zero-interest loan if you have been nice to them all these time.

The good thing about getting a loan from your inner circle is the relatively bigger sense of trust compared to asking them from strangers. You can collectively get more money with least amount of interest. But again, please be respectful; do your best to get the money working and keep your integrity by paying them back in full. A gift or two on the side afterward wouldn't hurt either. From your outer circle, you can knock on doors, advertise offline and online, and basically tell everyone that you have a great business idea but need a bit of a leg up. *As always, be mindful of stranger danger, and put everything down in writing as clearly and as legally as you can.*

Vendor financing. *Get someone who has vested interest in your investment to finance your initial capital.* Ask your future supplier, contractor, distributor, or anyone who will derive a benefit or commission in helping you. Think about this: if they believe in your product and service, they want to make money out of them once it is done, and they usually throw in some exclusivity clause so they become the sole handler of your product and service, and that is a massive market leverage for them. Not everyone wants to do it, but some of them may be visionary enough to see you through.

Joint ventures with existing business owners. This is about filling one another's gap. They usually need new product and service for their own clients, which is usually large enough for them to be wanting to have a joint venture and split the earning. *Not only will you have the initial capital, you will also gain credibility by association with the business owner, and that is a great leverage.* Contact the business owner in your industry, make the offer yourself so you'll be in control, but write it in from their point of view. Write it in a conversational manner. Be excited but avoid hype. Use a natural subject line as if you're sending it to a friend. If possible, give something of value in your first contact so they can see straightaway that you are not like others who only want to take and never give. If you stand out, you are more likely to be responded well.

Strategic partnership. *Get someone famous or with great credentials to work with you.* Never ever think celebrities are out of touch, and you don't have to start from the A-list; even minor celebrities in your industry can do wonders. What you do is to contact them via their agents; think always of how they will benefit from you and offer your product and service for free in exchange for their testimonials and marketing. Once you have it, people can see you're already a player in the industry, and no doubt, people with money with flock to you to join the party.

Government grant. Depending on where you live, government usually supports small businesses because it is the business owners who keep the country running, so they have vested interest in your project too. Of course, the bureaucracy can get in the way.

And yes, when I was applying for government grants, the delay and the unnecessary meticulous details they were asking frustrated me, not to mention the terms they imposed in exchange for the free money. But at the end of the day, *it is free money, and it only hurts a bit to get it.*

No money-down deal (advanced). You can seem to make money without money, but this takes a lot of financial intelligence. It is often called creative financing or no money down. Don't think it is a free lunch; you still need to take care of things that cost you effort, time, and energy. *Creative financing comes down to becoming a deal maker who solves problems for people, where orthodox methods are not sufficient. This is very research intensive. And you need access to the buyer and seller directly without an intermediary.*

When you see the opportunity, you find the buyer and seller, and you let the buyer pay for all the expenses plus profit to you as an intermediary. For example, in the real estate world, you can do a "flip" for a quick capital gain cash. If you are ever watching the property market and notice an occasional undervalued or foreclosed property, you would research the property carefully AND on-sell it to a buyer at a market value before YOU buy it yourself. Then negotiate a no-deposit terms in exchange for cash payment in the very near future. Then prior to settlement, let the buyer for the house buy it straight from you for at market value. The buyer of the house is happy; the seller of the house is happy. You come out with a profit to finance your investment, net of possible tax obligations. Often it is legitimate, but sometimes this kind of money-making scheme often involves benefiting on top of other's sufferings, bending the truth, and using deceit, so my recommendation is to either stick with using your private equity or think creatively without compromising your integrity.

✲✲✲

Right at the beginning, you have to equip yourself with a powerful tool of investment. And that tool is negotiation. *You have to accept that every business interaction is a negotiation. Not being conscious about it means losing in every single one of them.* And you must use your capital to its best potential. We have to learn whom we are negotiating with. One, speak in such a way that will appeal to your opponent's character. Two, be firm and persistent, but fair. Keep renegotiating until you have what you want. Ask more for less but be fairly fair. Always at least ask. If you will never ask, you will never get it. *But never negotiate on price alone. Good deals are never about price alone. The profit oftentimes can be found in the terms, not the price. Make sure you find out or make your own terms and conditions for mutual benefit.*

Don't be embarrassed to negotiate; you've worked hard for your money. Failing to negotiate means cutting your salary short. There are places you can't negotiate, but many are open to negotiation. And when negotiating, do it face-to-face whenever possible and bypass the salesman and get the sales manager or whoever has the final say. Demand to them that either the manager comes or you are out. Negotiation is a give-and-take process, but being in control of the process is the only way to be successful at it. Also, you need to be flexible and always know when to walk away. If you're more interested in buying than the seller is in selling, you won't win. *So you must know exactly what you want before the negotiation, ask fairly for more during the negotiation, and walk away as soon as your critical terms are compromised.*

❖ **Focus your investment on cash flow. Not capital gain. Not tax breaks.**

When deciding which particular investment you want to buy—meaning which property to buy, which business to buy, which shares to buy—focus solely on the cash flow and less on the possible capital gain, even lesser on the possible tax breaks. The worst investment is the one you buy just for the sake of receiving tax benefits. The better investment is to use momentum strategy for short-term traders who are in it for the capital gain. The best investment is the buy-and-hold strategy for long-term owners who are in it for the continuous cash flow.

The name of the game is to focus on cash flow and only consider capital gain as a bonus, if there is any. That way, you will make money irrespective of the economic condition. If your aim is to get capital gain, you must constantly be waiting and speculating for the best time to sell and to buy. Obviously, you don't want to be foolish and buy a clearly overpriced investment. The aim is not to profit from possible change in the value of the asset, but to ensure that your investment will produce constant cash flow. Capital gain is not cash flow. Although it can be transformed into cash flow, focus more on the real cash flow instead. Cash flow gives you freedom. So focus on the potential for passive income, and think capital gain only as a bonus, not the other way around. And do keep tax in mind, or let your accountant do that, but never let it interfere with your investment decision. When it comes to tax, focus on making the right decisions, then try to reduce the tax that goes along with it. And I'm talking about legally reducing your tax liability, not illegally evading paying tax.

The thing about capital gain is that, one, there are only limited occasions when you need to sell your assets and, two, unless your investment is in making capital gain, you cannot live on capital gains alone. So the *golden rule of financial freedom is to purchase the best investment possible and never ever sell it unless it is absolutely necessary.*

You may franchise or license your investment but never sell it. Don't sell any of your income-producing assets unless it is justifiable or you need a large amount of cash really desperately. If you have all the right insurances in place, such a need may not ever arise. There are few justifiable reasons to sell your investment. You may need to swap the current investment for a better one but are unable to afford it unless you sell the current investment. You may be reaching your good debt limit and need to sell some of your asset it to reduce your credit risk. Your investment may start to give you more headache than passive income. Whatever it is, use your good judgment and expert advice before you sell any of your investment.

Focusing on cash flow also gives you constant and relatively smaller incomes, which make you more humble than receiving a massive lump sum. We tend to be arrogant when we can make massive lump sum at one time. It will cloud our judgment. But if you are receiving a relatively small amount of money that increases slowly, you will grow as your money grows, and you will be more financially savvy. Focusing on cash flow also helps when the market crashes. You won't get nervous or emotional because the asset value may crash, but it has a lesser effect on your cash flow, and if you follow the strict requirement of choosing an investment, you may even make more money during down times.

Just a friendly reminder to keep documenting everything. By now you should have made your first investment. If you have made a careful and calculated investment, most likely you won't get a return in the first month or so. But chances are you may if you trade shares or set up a simple online business. Nevertheless, eventually you will receive your first return.

❖ DO NOT personally use the money that comes from your investment. Yet.

Just like when you plant a seed and it begins to grow a root, you wouldn't cut the root. This is the perfect time to make use the power of compounding interest. You are already financially secured from your job; you don't need to use more money. Use this money to reinvest or to invest further. This is the best time to use the income from your investment to create a system that allows automation. Right now, you are earning an active income, and your income must stay active for a while until your passive income can support your life. *So only once your system is set up and running, which will take a while, can you use the passive income for your personal use.*

❖ Create a system, and the system will set you free.

Once you've run your investment, you've actively participated in it for a while, and you know the working details of it, then you should now be able to see the big picture, the small pictures within, and every step involved on how to work things out. Whether you're working by yourself or have hired someone, you should know who should be responsible to do what by when, which has to go where by when, and how the investment works in flow diagram and in real life. You've done things on daily basis; you should be able to map things out.

Creating a system is hard work, complex, and time-consuming, so not everything there is to it is covered in this book. But nevertheless, it is very valuable, and the idea is quite simple and very doable. On the bigger scale, think of why big company directors do not have to be physically in the company every day for their company to earn them big dollars. It is because, one, they have *systems* set up within the company and, two, they *outsource* and lead their staff in their system, allowing everyone to know what is expected of them and how to do it. What you are about to do is the miniature version of their system.

Your system is basically the complete vision of your investment. It gives order, predictability, repeatability, and explanation of everything in your investment. Think of systemized business as a great product with a clear manual. Anyone should be able to read the manual and use the product efficiently. Your business is the product, and your system is the manual. And because your business is a product, you must work ON it, not IN it. The aim is to *make a system-dependent investment, not people-dependent investment.* Your financial structure must own your investment, but your involvement should be limited to being the owner. Once the system is up and running, your active participation is limited to periodical monitoring and working at the strategic level. If you have to be physically attending your investment to create your income, you are still working *in* it. You shouldn't be part of the product. You should be the owner of the product, working *on* your product to make it the best it can be. A system allows you to think about your business at the strategic level and not worrying about who is running it on a daily basis. And that's what the system is for. Think how big a leverage a system is.

It must be designed to provide a constant value to every part of your business both internally and externally. The system must provide uniformity. Having a working system equals automation. And automation equals passive income. Hard work? Of course. Work once and get passive income for life? Of course. Think as if you will be selling your business as a franchise. A franchisee must be able to study your system as an outsider and do what your business does with excellence. The franchisee knows everything about running their own franchise bought from you and little else about running your own franchise business. But that can only happen when your system is up and running.

Throw away the mentality that no one else can do things like you do or as perfectly as you do it. This is emotional thinking. You should know that perfection doesn't exist. And excellence done by others is as good as "perfection" done by yourself. You will have the opportunity to finalize things, but most of the work must be done by someone else. Sometimes, however, through great leadership, people can even do better things than you can do yourself. As a matter of fact, you must lead them to be better than you *because if you're the smartest in your business, you're in trouble because that is a threat to your system. Your system will then depend entirely on you to work.*

At the end of the day, a business comes down to two things: profit and leverage. And we are to maximize both. And the only way to do that is via a business system. The point is to employ people to do the menial and repeatable things to free you up so that you can keep doing important things and keeping yourself open to new things. You must spend most of your time on strategy and less on day-to-day action to get lots of results. And understand also that system creates value. When you create a working business without you in it, the business becomes very valuable. You are essentially creating a money making machine.

Now, every business is different, only you can tell what needs to be done. Some investments require little system involvement, especially if you can hire others like agents or managers to do the automation. Some investments require a massive and detailed business system. Regardless of your investment type, creating a system comes down to knowing and automating the following three things:

1) Business flow

This is about knowing the general flow of your investment from the start to a never-ending loop. *You must know in details and in steps how you would "process" your client from a complete stranger to your active marketer because the key is not only to make one sale but to have repeated and endless sales.* That's the whole thing of putting a system in place. You provide a consistent and trustworthy brand that people keep coming back to you and keep referring others to come to your business. *Getting a new customer is more costly than keeping the old one, so your system must be dependable.* Most businesses do not have a system that keeps their customers on the loop. They say good-bye as soon as the financial transaction is done.

Your system must be as simplified as possible. It should come down to bullet points, exact step by step of what things need to be done and how to do it. And it must be easily accessible. Don't create complex, jargon-filled manuals with boring policies and procedures. Make it an interesting how-to guide.

2) *Test and Measure*

You have to know whether your investments are doing what they are supposed to be doing and at an acceptable level. You have to know whether your employees are doing what they supposed to be doing and at an acceptable level. *You must set up a system of numbers, testing and measuring every part of your investment.* When you do, you will know how to minimize your cost and risk and to maximize your efficiency and effectiveness.

Once the system is up and running, not only will you automatically have the customers data, you will also have your employees data, your business data, your suppliers data, your accounting data, and many other things. Your system needs to give you as much Key Performing Indicator (KPI) as possible on every aspect of your business. Don't worry about profit; it will come when everything else has been taken care of. You must get down and dirty to know what's going on in your investment. How many customers come in through the door offline and online? How many of them end up purchasing your goods or services? How did they find out about your business? Why didn't they purchase anything when they were in your shop?

And at the same time, your system must allow you to experiment and get result from your experiment. If you put ads on the yellow pages, if you try new trading or computer software, if you renovate your property, if you split test a website, you need to know how all these affect your investment in real numbers.

3) *Accountability*

You have to establish who does what to a point that if anything goes wrong, you know who is accountable. Everyone has to know what they're doing and expected to do. This is also to protect you if someone argues that you didn't tell them to do certain things. Trust me, debating who said what or did what is pointless. Your business must be dependent on the system and not on the people. It must not be depended on one particular employee. *Each employee's work must be replicable, or at least quickly replaced by someone new.* At all times, every personnel must know what they have to do and know what to do if they don't know something.

This is done by the creation of various how-to manuals. If your business makes coffee, you have to have an operational manual detailing step-by-step how to make great coffee. It is so detailed and practical to a point that a stranger can do a similar job your employee is doing by just looking at the operation manual. So if someone is sick, their job can be replaced by anyone else in your business. The only exception to this rule is when you have the highly skilled employees as part of your team, and the system will be quite limited but still necessary.

No one can detail an accountant's or lawyer's work if they happen to be on your team as the work involves good judgment. Nevertheless, your system must still not be dependent on the people. Your business must be then quite large too so you can afford multiple high-skilled professionals to replace one another. But your system still has to support the work transfer process.

Document everything. This is the key to automation. Automation is only possible if everybody knows and is willing to do the right thing. Delegate and automate. The instructions must be available, functional, and easily understood by everyone. The instructions must be specific and detailed for it to be duplicable. And in addition to text, you can put illustrations and videos. You must get yourself or together with your employees to document every single step they do in order to do their job. You know you've done this successfully if when one of your employees calls in sick, the system replaces the work with ease by following your documentation. Although this event itself will be documented, but unless you monitor your system, you wouldn't even know about it, and your investment will still run smoothly as usual. The same thing must also happen if you lose your supplier; the system can replace them with ease by following your documentation. Do this for every *major* and *minor* task. *Write as much and as specific as you can.* When I was working at the supermarket, the wall was filled with documentation and illustration on how to do routines; even somebody from the other department could easily perform what I was doing.

✻✻✻

Step-by-Step Fundamentals of System Creation

Step 1 – Find out and write every task in your business that needs to be done, which are currently done by yourself or others in your business. To make things easier, write it as everyone does their daily business. Do this for at least a month but preferably three months to get a quarter average of your business activities.

Step 2 – Put all the tasks under different headings. As you collect your tasks during your daily business, separate the to-do list to frequency: daily, weekly, monthly, and miscellaneous. And to functionality: accounting, marketing, etc. Write as much and as specific as you can.

Step 3 – Separate yourself from the tasks. At the end of the period, find out from all the lists anything that is repetitive and teachable. You must have the fewest things to do to allow new things in your business. Don't be emotional; be objective, then separate and put as much tasks as you can to your assistant so that your list only contains a list of important things that you cannot delegate.

DO NOT outsource strategy and planning, monitoring performance, relationship building, product development, system creation, business finances, and things you love to do.

You must never fully let go of your business, especially the sales department. You personally must be able to sell your products and services and have control over money coming into your business.

Step 4 – Document everything and start to create your system. For each to-do task, you have to create explanation and show your assistant how to do it. For each system, create the what, why, when, where, and how and summarize the steps at the end. The point is that they must be able to train themselves and others with your system. Your instructions must be as simple and as specific as possible so that anyone can just look at it and do things the way you like it.

Step 5 – Update, protect, and make the system limited but easily accessible by your staff. As you make progress and learn from your failures, your system must reflect both. Your system must also be continually backed up. Make sure your staff has an easy but limited access just to serve their roles. But do let your staff help you or train them with system creation specific to their roles.

***

Keep doing this, nurture it, and eventually, your business will passively run. All you have to do is monitor and control the performance while focusing your work on the strategic level. Now, a business may require various systems like human resource system, accounting and finance system, payment system, marketing system, and other systems. So there must also be a master system above all these. Don't worry, you will not be overwhelmed. Because you started small, you'll grow with your business. All these don't happen overnight. It happens over months and years.

But system can only work if you outsource the tasks within the system. As you will find out, there are too many important as well as menial things that need to be done, and you need others to help you with those menial things so you are free to do the important things. *Outsourcing is about finding cost-effective help with minimum input from the owner.* And they can only work once the system is set up and you know exactly what you need others to do. When it comes to outsourcing, you may need both local and virtual assistants. The two complement each other. It is always risky to hire someone, even more when they are not even in the same country, but it can be managed. And without them, you will forever be trapped in your business.

Specific to your investment, here are some of the examples of system usage:

- If you are into investing in property, most of your automation already come from your agent. Just make sure you still retain control. An agent's interest isn't always necessarily yours. There are various things you can demand your agents to do to make sure they are doing the right thing. Once a year, preferably spontaneous, get together with your property agent to do inspection together. You'll find out then what kind of agents they are. Those who thoroughly check on things or those who are just good tick-box tickers. In terms of system, all you need to create is an information system. It is critical that you have an information system, allowing you to know what needs to be done regulary, and have easy and accurate access to intel on your current and next purchase. You have to know why it is a good property or how likely you will get a tenant. And research must be such a breeze that you can hire someone to do it because the system tells you where to go exactly and what kind of intel to get.

- If you are into shares trading, most of your automation already come from your trading software, but it is also still critical that you have an information system, allowing you to have easy and accurate access to intel on your current and next purchase. Your system has to tell you when to buy, when to sell, how to avoid loss, how to execute strategies, when your options are due, etc. Try to automate all these.

- If you are into commercial business, especially offline, you need a system to run everything. From contacting supplier, handling customers, dealing with accounting, finance, marketing, etc. If you have an online business, the system is relatively simpler. You'll be amazed at how you practically have software for everything, to create a website, to set up a secure shopping cart, and everything else to get your online business up and running practically automatic. Duplication is very easy on the Internet. Now, business system is relatively the hardest to create, but your hard work also comes with the highest potential for growth compared to other investments.

- If you are into licensable artistic work, your system is mainly in production and marketing even though you may have an agent or manager. Your system must always tell you what to do next, how to get certain effects/equipment for your art, how to outsource other artists, how to land opportunites, and everything else you do to deliver your art to the end customers. And just as you would with properties, you cannot rely 100% on your agents and managers to act in your best interest. Always be in control.

❖ Once you have a passive income, diversify and multiply.

Once you have your system in place, you will derive passive income out of it. Again, don't touch the passive income just yet, but use it this time to diversify. *Diversify either within the asset category or among asset categories.* You've done it once; surely you can do it again. If you're in property business, either keep buying more properties or try to do other investments. You just have to multiply your passive income. One may not be much, but think when you have five of them. Discipline is a must as always. Don't break the chain of investment. Don't cut short the power of compounding interest. Your patience will pay off. But you can only diversify when you can afford to do it. Most people diversify first and that is risky.

When your multiple assets have all been automated and the healthy passive income is enough to support your life, you may now have the choice to drop your full-time job completely, if you hadn't done it. Only when you have multiple incomes AND your income covers your expenses can you use the excess money for personal use. And guess what, by this stage, you are financially free! Go celebrate, share, and be very, very grateful! Remember to keep controlling your expenses as you grow with your income. Never ever let your expenses exceed your income again. Other than that, your time is all yours. Your life is no longer bounded by money. You will thank yourself. Your family will thank you. And I'm sure you will be a much better person by now. And I'm very happy for you!

❖ The ten most common reasons why people fail financially.

You will undoubtedly meet temporary setbacks in this journey. And when it comes to financial failures, it is like anything else in life. It is easier to prevent than to fix. So prepare heavily. These are the ten most common reasons why people fail financially.

- **Lack of due dilligence, planning, and research.** We only make plans in our heads, and we think that's enough. We stop learning and become complacent with our education and research. We choose the wrong investment. We are not in control of what will happen to our investment. We are surprised by the outcome. We delegate to the wrong people. We rely on others to do things we are supposed to do ourselves. We pick the wrong financing for our investment. We end up wasting a lot of time, money, and energy to mitigate our mistake.

- **Lack of support.** There is no common, shared, and accepted goal. There is no cohesiveness of a team. We don't get the support and commmitment from our partner, our family, and our experts. When we are not supporting each other, investment can be wasteful, and relationships can be broken.

- **Lack of protection.** We fail to realize and prioritize what is important. Insurances are not set in place. We show off our financial wealth.

- **Lack of good health.** We fail to maintain our holistic health. We are physically and mentally unwell to assess things and make good decisions.

- **Fail to act.** We let fear and doubt take over instead of research and acting on opportunities. Or we wait for opportunities to come to us instead of creating one up ourselves. We retreat at the first sign of difficulty. We let the cost of our education stop our education.

- **Being emotional instead of being rational and analytical.** We hate the person we're dealing with and let it hinder us from our investment. Or maybe we haven't upgraded our communication skills yet so that we sound like we're greedy every time we negotiate. We follow our friend's advice on investing. We fall into temptation of purchasing a luxury instead of thinking of the usefulness and the affordability of it.

- **Being impatient, being late, or being indecisive.** We rush, we delay, or we keep changing our minds and we are unable to make a good judgment. And when we do any of these, we are more likely to make the wrong decision, and therefore, mistakes can easily happen. It is very tempting to rush, to procrastinate, and to follow herd. And it is hard when we are cornered to make a decision. But generally, if we have done enough research and planning, we should know what the best decision is.

- **Ungrateful.** Our personality is not conducive to our investment. We forget God, our family, our clients, and those who have helped us along the way. Or we don't give them fair remuneration for their work. People can be evil if we don't treat them right. Be a good and grateful person; that's your best guarantee.

- **Force majeure.** Disasters strike, and there is nothing we can do about it. We can only rebuild what's been destroyed.

- **A compulsory life lesson.** Despite our very best human effort, we still fail because we are not perfect. It just has to happen, no explanation, and there is nothing we can do except to learn from it and move on.

Remember that money-making is a serious game; anyone can win or lose anytime. But if you have protected yourself, seven months is plenty of time for you to restart if you happen to suffer from significant financial hardship. So every time you know you're in danger, you can use that money, but always replenish that money first before getting back. Again, it's about taking control of your financial wealth, and if you play it right, it's not risky. It even protects you from other risks.

You're off to your journey with a massive head start. Be very grateful about that. People who did it through trial and error suffered significantly. And knowing all these, you don't have to. The next part is the hands-on approach to your life project. By possessing all these knowledge, what else is there to do but to act?

THE ACTION OF FINANCIAL FREEDOM

If you're like me, then you will probably read this section before the first two. Learn from my mistake—don't do it. You won't even understand it. Re-read the first two parts until you fully understand what holistic financial freedom is.

This section is only designed to assist you in implementing the combination of mind-set and strategy in real-life situation. This is where you make deals and take real action. I'll show you how someone with zero financial wealth— or worse, in debt—can achieve financial freedom, so you don't really have an excuse not to do this. Treat this as your most exciting DIY project.

Notice that this is the shortest part of the book because once you've fully grasped the first two sections, you'll easily move to action. Chances are you won't even need this section, but not everyone is the same. So consider this section as a three-wheeled bicycle for your journey.

There is no way I can determine your starting point or appreciate the complexity of your life, but for everyone's sake, we will have two generalized starting points, then both will converge into one same journey toward financial freedom. I would suggest that you read them all even though some part may not be directly relevant to your situation.

General Starting Point 1

❖ **You're under eighteen years of age, and you're living comfortably.**

You have to be in school and finish it, no excuse. Think not of what you have to do. Think of what you will miss out if you don't attend school. Think of the invaluable friends you would never get to meet otherwise. Think of the invaluable life lessons that will shape your character. Think of the impact of schooling for the rest of your life. It may not be your best experience in life, but the problems you encounter in school and how you solve them determine your future. I learned a lot about life, much more than the academics while I was at school, and these experiences led my life. As a matter of fact, I've forgotten majority of the academics, but I still use the life and the social skills to this day.

If you're under fifteen and your parents are taking good care of you, close this book, go to school, go out have fun with your friends, and worry not about tomorrow. Don't bother knowing all these just yet. The fun you're having now can never be replaced anywhere in the future. The bonds and the sweet memories you have with your friends will stay for the rest of your life. And they are critical to your mental development throughout your life.

Going back to the topic. Right now, you must start reading books on investment in your free time and attend free seminars the gurus run. But don't buy the program they are offering unless you understand totally about it and confident that you can make good judgment on it and your decision is verified by experts, because there are only few gems out there. About 99.9% of them will end up selling you something. But at the same time, they always provide relatively valuable stories and advice at the beginning of their seminars to entice you to buy. Write it down, and learn from it. It's a good starting point.

I would recommend you to be independent early on. Start looking for a casual or part-time job while you're still at school. By getting a job before you even graduate from high school, you're ahead in terms of life, experience, and résumé value than your peers. You'll understand how it feels to have a boss, how it feels to have job responsibility, and how it feels to serve both good and bad customers. All these prepare you and toughen you for the life ahead. And once you have a job, learn to save. Start the discipline of applying the "pay yourself first" concept, and start putting aside money for others.

This is also a good time to plan for your life ahead. I didn't know what to do when I graduated from high school. I even spent the first year of college studying the wrong degree. So for you, I want you to learn from my mistake and visualize clearly what your life will be like five years after you graduated, where you will be, what you will do, what you will know about life, how your finances will look like. You must have goals in life and start early because time is very precious.

You have to have a destination in life. You cannot be idle and waste time. Maybe you want to pursue your athletic or artistic talents. Maybe you want to start your investment now. Whatever it is, explore the world and discover it yourself. See what interests you the most. There are unlimited fun, noble, and fulfilling things in this world that you can see and experience that may awaken your inner self. Once you find something you like, hold on to it tight and think how financial freedom will give the time for you to enjoy the things you really enjoy. Remember that you are now an adult who must accept the consequences of your choices in life, both good and bad. And finally, don't ruin your dream with stupid things like alcohol and drugs abuse.

A summary of the to-do list in steps:

✓ Re-read the first section and be wealthy first. Internalize and make wealth mind-set your character then depart from the point of wealth today.

✓ Be grateful. Many may never have access to information in this book in their lives. Think thousands of reasons to be grateful and send it to God. Let Him know you're grateful by being positive in life and by sharing this gratitude and positivity with everyone.

✓ Attend school faithfully. Learn as much as you can. Make as much friends as you can. You'll never know who ends up doing what, even the geeky and the bitchy ones. But pick your close friends carefully.

✓ Attend free seminars, read books on personal finance and on your choice of investment in your free time. Either buy them or read them free from your library.

✓ Explore the world. Find your passion trigger, try new things. But avoid alcohol and drugs abuse. No one grows up willing to be an addict, but some of us will, and it will destroy your life beyond your imagination.

✓ Create your personal goals based on your passion and your meaning of life. Write it down, and put it in a place where you can remind yourself of them every day. You're on your way to find yourself, so it's ok to change goals, as long as your life always has a positive direction to go to.

✓ Try to get a job and start paying yourself first, give some as charity, and don't touch your savings. Let the compound interest do its job.

✓ Make a habit of giving early on; your return will be more than any compound interest can give.

General Starting Point 2

❖ **You're an adult, but you think you have nothing at all. You are absolutely destitute.**

You may be a refugee. You're living under the $2 line. You don't have a home. You've lost all your families. Or you may have just suffered a massive business loss, been through a painful divorce, spent money carelessly, or anything. To a lesser degree, you may be just a college student with little cash or a kid with less fortunate background. Whatever it is, if you're reading this book, one fact remains: you still have the most precious gift you will ever have—your own life. And remember that there is always someone worse than you overcoming worse things. So you really have no excuse to give up because you still have so much wealth. A living person cannot be valued by money. The richest person in the world cannot buy an extra second for his or her life, and you still have plenty. So even in your darkest hours, never ever think that your life is no longer has any meaning.

I don't claim to understand your situation. But you don't need sympathy or self-pity; you need help from yourself and others. Sympathy won't get you anywhere. Re-read the mind-set section and internalize it in your mind. This is the time when you must understand the mind-set of success and apply it in your life. You are not ruined until you think you are. The limit there is, is only the one your mind creates. And hope is only lost the moment you give up on yourself. Don't think yourself as a victim but a survivor. Survivors go on with their lives after a tragedy whereas victims continue to wallow in self-pity.

I'm sure it's not easy, but keep applying your wealth mind-set while you keep finding any means necessary for you to survive. Go back to your parents, be on welfare temporarily, beg for money, go to charity offices or any other refuge, or go to nearby churches. A real church is always open for physically and spiritually destitute people.

Once you know that you will survive another day, meaning you have eaten, have a temporary bed, a temporary roof over your head, then be grateful; many won't even make it to where you are. Never forget to dream even at this stage of your life. It may be hard; you may be filled with anger, regret, and frustration. But remember, success is the best and sweetest revenge for all the painful memories of the past. If you're angry, turn it into energy to propel you forward. Think to yourself that your situation doesn't make sense; because you already have the wealth and what it takes to control your reality. So now, prove to yourself that you can succeed in this life.

Never think there isn't much else to do if you absolutely have no financial power at all. It doesn't mean you don't have anything. Stop monetizing everything. Your wealth comes from within, not by possession.

And now, because you know that you are wealthy, you are fit to get a job. You have something precious to offer others. Start looking for a job. Any job, but preferably the one that you like and passionate about. You may have excuses and reasons to say to yourself that you are not fit to get a job. But persistence, confidence, and determination play a more important role than what you actually know. And all these are things you already have inside you. Don't be lazy. There is really no excuse for you not to be working.

Polish you résumé, do volunteer work while you're unemployed, and keep searching for openings either formally or informally. Formally, you may be replying to ads or sending your résumé through your agent. Informally, you can tell everyone you know that you're looking for a job. Or better yet, talk to businesses directly. Ring them, go to their offices, ask them if they need someone to do the menial jobs so they can focus on the important stuff. Be genuinely interested in helping them, and people will appreciate it. Focus on them. Think and explain to them how your service can be beneficial to their business. I was door knocking for a job once myself. When I finally got the job, I asked my employer why they decided to hire me. They said it was because of my genuine confidence that I could help them. Mind you, I was without the proper academics required for the role.

Once you have a job, no matter what it is, no matter how low you get paid for, be very, very grateful because for every opening, there are others who compete against you. That alone is your small victory. And you'll be pleased to know that once you are employed, it is much easier to get a better job compared to applying it as an unemployed. Now, pay yourself first, and again, make your gratitude evident by sharing some of your wealth. It is counter logical to give out money when you don't even have enough for yourself. But this is about the spiritual side of money. Don't give it unwillingly, or it will be pointless. Give with a cheer. Giving out of poverty is much more rewarding than giving out of riches. If you are in no position to give at all, then postpone your charity.

It is also the time for you to have an address. So start renting in a humble residence. But consider also your workplace and how efficient your travel would be. But if you have no other option, then take it. I know it's not your home, but the feeling of having a roof over your head is a good feeling to have.

A summary of the to-do list in steps:

✓ Re-read the first section and be wealthy first. Internalize and make wealth mind-set your character then depart from the point of wealth today.

✓ Be grateful to God that you are still alive and still able to read this book. Stay positive because being negative can only make things worse. Remember that you are not a victim; you are a survivor.

✓ Seek help from anywhere you can to help you to survive. God helps those who help themselves. Make sure you can get food, clothing, and shelter.

✓ Once your life is relatively stable, get any kind of job. Be creative in approaching businesses. Think of how they would like to get help from you. And upgrading your job after you get a job is easier than applying for a job when you're unemployed.

✓ If you fail to get a job, re-read the first two parts of this book. The skill you use to sell product or service is the same skill you can use to sell your service to businesses.

✓ Pay yourself first and share some of your wealth to charity or others in need to make sure that you've created an endless loop of wealth.

✓ Try to get a stable home address. This will help you with lots of things.

❖ **You're now working. It doesn't pay well, but at least you have a stable income.**

It's good to start small because your financial freedom will start small too. This is the moment when you need to start learning. Regardless of your job, you must purchase a journal, an empty book. This is one of the most valuable investments you will ever make. If you've gone through a bad experience, you write it down. Dump your painful memories and use it to push you forward. When you have ideas or light bulb moment from your subconscious mind, you write it down. Write your failures, your achievements, your private information, your financial plan. When your head gets big, remember your failures and humble yourself. When you're having a hard time, remember your achievements and motivate yourself. When you have no idea of where to go, go back to your financial plan and redirect your focus.

Write your job experience on the journal. Learn why you are needed, why someone is willing to pay you to do your job. Keep working while learning about business, instead of focusing only to get things done as your boss wants you to. Ask why and find out why. When I was "working" in a supermarket, I didn't really work there. I was merely enrolled into a traineeship. I learned firsthand how a big supermarket is managed—the logistic, the payroll, the inventory management, and a general understanding of how the supermarket works. I questioned things and I found out about them. What I was learning was business skills. I don't run a supermarket now, but I still use the skills I learned there today. So for now, your goal is to be excellent at your job and to seek promotion. You must at least be in a managerial position. The skills you will learn are very valuable for yourself in the future.

This is the time when you must implement a good financial habit. For the next one full month, record every income and expenses. Round up smallest expenses. But the more specific, the better. Don't spend more than you earn. Fill in your budget. Start creating your financial freedom map. Know where you have to go from here. Start committing the thirty-minute rule. Start to network with the people in your industry and in your choice of investment.

Maintain your "pay yourself first" and your charity work. Now that you have a job, control your expenses and make sure you are financially secure. Start filling your seven months' savings account, and then your investment account. You're in the better position already than people who may earn more but whose lives are so hectic they practically turn themselves into robots. They run in the treadmill of life. They're busy, sure, but they are not going anywhere. They are not doing what you're doing. They don't study their job. They don't study anything. They're clueless, but you're not.

A summary of the to-do list in steps:

✓ Be grateful that you have a job. That is something to be positive about. Be grateful that you go and come back home from your job safely every day. If you're sick or happen to be in an accident, be grateful you're not dead. If you happen to be dead, then be grateful you already know and acknowledge the true and living God, who owns this world and the afterlife, and who will gladly take care of you.

✓ Purchase your journal. This is your first investment. Keep it safe. Keep it close by. Write everything down. Reflect on it every day.

✓ Maintain the thirty-minutes-a-day commitment.

✓ Create your budget. Find out where you are and where you want to go in your financial freedom map.

✓ Maintain "pay yourself first" and your charity work. You should have started accumulating your seven months' worth of expenses.

✓ Do a general research and choose your first choice of investment. Read on topics associated with your first investment. Read at least five books. Study them and get the main points out of every single book. If you are certain and can afford it, you can start purchasing real education program.

✓ Be nice and professional to every customer you serve, to your colleagues, and to your boss. There are numerous stories where people are hired for a better job by the clients they were serving previously. And as always, be good and diligent at your job and seek promotion to at least a managerial level. Handle office politics, don't deny their existence wherever you are.

❖ **You're now working, earning a stable and more income, but you made a wrong decision of purchasing things that do not appreciate in value. You live paycheck by paycheck, and you feel like you're running in a rat race.**

This may be the starting point for quite a number of us. You may have a job; you may have found love and may be married, have kids, with a mortgage and other debts. You're living paycheck by paycheck. And it seems money is never enough no matter how hard or how many jobs you have. You may not hate your job, but you would prefer to do something else.

And usually, you may, by now, have purchased lots of things that decrease in value, therefore reducing your cash flow. Worse, you went into debt to get it. You bought a car, a yacht, a TV with debt. Or you may have purchased a house and stuck with the mortgage for the rest of your life. You are officially the member of the Rat Race club, the treadmill of life. But you've learned your mistake, and you're ready to fix it.

Worry not. You should know better by now that you are at least financially secure and way ahead of the majority of people. Start by getting rid of all the bad debt you have with the first one that is most emotionally attached to you. Then get rid of the rest one by one. Mortgage is the only one you may keep. But even with this, consider going back to renting and make your home your first investment. You should have saved the seven months' savings by now and some on your investment account. But never use this money to repay your loan. Use the rest of your budget to do it. Get help. There is a mentality of "coolness" that makes you think you don't need anybody to succeed. Successful people know that the key to their success is to get other people's help. So seek professional advice on how to get rid of your debt.

By now you'll be living comfortably; you are financially secured, but your income is still largely active income. Talk to your partner and kids about financial freedom and get them committed with the plan. Explain to them how this is a team effort. Talk about preserving or even enhancing the comfortable life you all are living now. Once you accumulate the seven months worth of expenses and you have accumulated surplus on your investment account, you can start buying real education programs specific to your investment. You have to obtain specialized, focused, and detailed knowledge of your investment. You have to know exactly why the property, or the share, or the business you're buying is a good investment. What specific criteria and validations do you use to justify them? What specific intel that you use to support your decision? What do the experts say about your investment? How do you work out the predictable cashflow? You have to know all these, but don't start investing just yet.

A summary of the to-do list in steps:

✓ Be grateful. You have already started your journey. You are financially secured. Imagine those who don't know what to eat for tomorrow. Always be grateful to God and make your gratitude evident in your life. Stay positive; share your wealth.

✓ Create your internal and external team. Create a covenant with your family that you will support each other all the way through.

✓ Get rid of all the bad debt ASAP. Seek professional help. Ring the company for help. Don't take another loan to cover a loan. Work diligently to put aside money to clear all your debt on top of your routine "pay yourself first" and charity work. Aim to be as debt-free as possible.

✓ Start learning the technicality of your investment. You have to have real, thorough, and complete understanding of your investment. Remember, reality is ever validating your education and is not very forgiving. Attend seminars, buy programs, hire mentors specific to your choice of investment.

✓ Simultaneously, start making thorough research on relevant insurances you might need to protect yourself, your family, and your investment.

✓ Seek expert advice now in regard to your choice of investment and the best financial structure for your circumstances.

✓ Start gathering your equity in your investment account and think creatively to gather enough initial capital to make the first purchase of your investment.

✓ If you think you've failed in anything, re-read the first two parts of the book again.

✓ If you have a large mortgage, either stay at home and refinance to reduce your mortgage payment to a minimum or consider renting your home to someone else for it to be your first investment while you are living in a humbler rent. That way, your tenant pays your mortgage, and even after paying your rent, you will still have a little passive income.

WARNING

You must have your savings account filled with seven months' worth of conservative expenses, your investment account enough to purchase your first investment, AND you must be technically savvy on your first choice of investment prior to proceeding.

❖ **You're now bad-debt free, or you may only have a mortgage and ready to start your investment.**

At this stage, your mind-set must already be your character, and your strategies are fixed in your mind and written somewhere. This is the interesting time to invest. You may feel overwhelmed by your investment obligations. You don't have to. Start small, trust wisely, and delegate your tasks. Treat your investment as a part-time business, then slowly and gradually progress to full-time businesses that produce multiple passive incomes. Use the money in your investment account to pay people who can help you. Keep writing things down as you meet people, as you calculate things, as you make mistakes and successes.

Yes, the feeling of letting your hard-earned money go into your investment isn't that pleasant, but you know what you're doing now. That money will give much more return to you. Be actively involved with your investment. Now is the time for a hands-on learning about running your investment in real life. Study it. Study why it works or why it doesn't work. And early on, start envisioning how you can create your investment system. There will be unexpected expenses and frustrating people to deal with, but you will have fun along the way. Remember, you cannot do this dreadfully and expect something nice out of it.

A summary of the to-do list in steps:

✓ Be very grateful now that you are able to make an investment. Many don't even have a clue what an investment is. Stay positive because you will meet negative people along the way. Keep sharing because you will now experience how things will come back to you. People whom you have helped before may offer something useful to your investment. The possibility is endless, but what goes around will come around.

✓ Sit down somewhere quiet. Involve your partner or people you can trust. Take time to really think things through. Get serious, because thinking is where the wealth is. Until you can visualize your wealth through your investment, you will not attain your wealth physically. Draw diagrams, predict outcomes, find gaps, create to-do list, merge the expert advice you've gathered so far. While you're doing this, you're automatically communicating with your subconscious mind which will give you ideas and answers whenever you are stuck.

✓ Make thorough calculation and practice a lot. DO NOT make any investment at all until you know exactly what the possible outcomes will be and exactly what the steps are in between now and later. Even little things you don't know now may cost you lots later. Then when you are confident, make your first investment and be actively involved in it. But never rush or delay your investment, you will only create waste.

✓ If you choose property as your first investment, I would strongly suggest using a simple "buy, hold, and rent it out" strategy. Gather intel on the property you're about to purchase, on the local government about details and possible regulation changes, and on finance. No renovation. No subdivision. And no building. This is about starting small. You can handle headaches as you grow but maybe not on your first attempt. Use an agent as part of your automation strategy. But never take your agent for granted. Never think your agent will solve all your problems. Be aware of what they do and how to verify it.

✓ If you choose share trading as your first choice of investment, start analyzing intel from your sources and do live paper trading. Use live data but don't use real money, then analyze your success and mistakes on paper. Use virtual trading early on if available before doing the real trades. Aim to create a delta neutral portfolio for a start. Research for the best software to automate your trading. Keep in touch with your broker.

✓ If you choose commercial business (offline or online) as your first choice of investment, start looking for premise or domain, start creating or sourcing products, start looking for suppliers, and start thinking of marketing, accounting, and finance. Start setting up and be committed to your business website. Start networking with other people in your industry.

✓ If you choose licensable artistic work as your first choice of investment, make sure you network with other artists. If you are creating a band, get a full commitment from everyone. Define in writing, the terms and conditions before you create your band. Communication is very essential. Practice long until you are really comfortable. Then start approaching restaurants, clubs, or anywhere else that has a live music event. You can even try to approach places that do not have it and suggest to them how they will benefit from your art. Start with playing covers then create your own songs. If you are a programmer, start collaborating with others and create your software. Find out how to protect your work on the Internet. Start selling them and always try to get feedback from your customers.

✓ If you are writing a book, make thorough research on your topic and on your competitors. Make sure your topic is on demand and you can provide a unique view on it. Once you have your final manuscript, research and decide whether you want to go through the traditional publishing route or the self-publishing route. Query the first five publishers, not all of them at once. That allows you to learn from your mistake, if any. If you drop it all at once, you have no one else to query to. And reality is not very friendly. A no the first time is usually a real no, unless you can really convince them the second time.

Make sure you understand the contract before you sign it with any publishers. If you self-publish, make sure your copyright is protected. Make sure you know how to do and who will do every single little thing that is involved with a book production. And make sure your marketing plan is as solid as a rock. Self-publishing means you have to market your book yourself, and it can be difficult. If you want to use the service of a vanity publisher, my advice is to research and fully understand the pros and cons. It may or may not work for you. The quality of the book may be poor, the royalty may not be fair, the control of the book may be lacking, etc.

✓ Purchase all the relevant and necessary types of insurance. Shop around and make sure you know exactly what is covered and what is not.

✓ Start drafting your system, write all the steps you're doing as you go along.

✓ Plan how to respond to possible failures ahead. If you do fail and become emotional, re-read the first two sections of this book again.

❖ **Your investment is running and eventually making you money.**

It is not very often that you make money in your first month or even couple of months. This is where you must keep injecting money from your investment account and from your active income. But once your investment does produce income, the only thing left to do now is to systemize, duplicate, and diversify. You've done it once; surely, you can do it again. If you have purchased a property, buy the second one. If you have traded in share market in your country, try different commodities and derivatives or try to trade on different countries. If your commercial business has made you money, buy another business. If your music has produced a single, create an album. If you've written a book, write another one.

And as you do all that, you'll notice that certain things are just repetitions others can do for you. This is the time you must create a system for your investment. The time to do this can range from a couple of months to years in order to get it right. It's not easy. But it sets you free. Once you have a working system, only then can you diversify on your asset class or branch out to other types of assets.

A summary of the to-do list in steps:

✓ Be very grateful now that you're making money on your investment. Many go through trial and error without knowing what you know now, and the loss may have been very costly to their lives. Stay positive now that you are ahead of the population who rely solely on their job for income. Keep sharing your joy of wealth.

✓ Upgrade your investment. Do more complex and more rewarding investments while patiently and diligently creating a fully working system. Take your time. Detail every step. Outsource and hire the right people at the right time, for the right duration. Test and measure everything.

✓ Try leaving your investment for a couple of days or weeks and when you get back, address things that do not work. You will learn a lot from it. A good test if your system is working is when you go for a holiday for six months, you come back wealthier than when you left.

✓ Duplicate your effort and diversify your investment to other types of assets. Repeat the cycle. You've done similar things; try new things.

❖ **Your investment has multiplied, and you have multiple sources of passive income. You've made it!**

It's been long and tough. To reach this point, it might take you years. Frustrating and disappointing at times. But you definitely had fun, and it is safe to say you've now become a new person. It takes a tremendous amount of courage for you to be financially free. You challenged the conventional thinking, you didn't pay attention to those who tried to put you down, you took calculated risks, you acted on your ideas, and now you have reaped what you have sown. It's a fact that you are a better person than you were at the start of your journey. For all those I commend you. Appreciate the journey more than the destination you have arrived in. But rejoice also that your passive income is now more than your regular expenses and your investment is supporting your life. Congratulations! Remember to appreciate and acknowledge those who helped you along the way. And to give back and to share. Remember to enjoy the joy of wealthy living.

A summary of the to-do list in steps:

✓ Be very, very grateful. You are in the minority of those who are financially free and have more time, energy, and resources to address your passion, to make real changes to the world, to be the best person you can be.

✓ Now that money comes with little effort, your responsibility to keep giving is even more. You have the financial power; use it for the good, for it shall return to you. Never compromise your integrity; your short-term pleasure can never pay for your long-term consequences.

✓ Address every aspect of your wealth. Remember to keep having fun! You have all the time in this life to have and to share it. Enjoy the freedom! Do again something that you have done at the very start of this journey: enjoy every breath of your life.

I hope you now realize that achieving financial freedom is really possible for you because it is about finding and following a successful formula; something everyone can do. And the more you know about the big picture, and at the same time, the very small manageable steps, the easier it becomes. Let's now cover some of the remaining questions on financial freedom.

Q&A Session

These are some of the common questions I get asked when people talk about all things financial freedom. Just little bits here and there to complete your understanding. The following are only my humble opinions.

Why do you share it with us if this works? Everybody else will keep it to themselves unless it doesn't work and try to sell it to others.

Well, I'm not everybody else. If everyone else is doing the same thing, it doesn't mean you should too. I think for myself before I do anything. And I practice what I preach. I believe, and many others believe this too, that wealth is unlimited and the joy of wealth is meant to be shared to everyone. I appreciate the currency of love much more than the currency of money. And that's why I think everyone deserves to know what you already know now.

Should I start a business from scratch, or should I buy others' businesses or franchises?

It depends. The mistakes you'll make if you start from scratch will be invaluable lessons to yourself, but buying others' businesses/franchises does give you some kind of shortcut. You will be buying your own customers and equipment at a discount. So basically, your choice is to either buy a business at a premium price, which already has the potential to be automatable, or you can start with or buy an underperforming business and transform it yourself. I've heard success stories from both scenarios. I personally would rather build my business and be the one who sells businesses and franchises to others.

Regardless of your choice, make sure you negotiate hard on anything, especially early on. Then get your accountant to check it thoroughly. Get them to focus on cash flow in the past, present, and future, both if you are starting out from zero or acquiring somebody else's business. And if you buy a pre-owned business that is not a franchise, get the previous owner to teach you for the first few months as part of the deal. With franchise, you usually have an ongoing support system you can use.

When should I buy a home of my own?

When you can afford it. Buying it with cash would be too much for most of us. On one side, a home is a wealth liability because it does not produce income. On the other, a home is an asset because it will increase in value, and the feeling of having a home is invaluable. So like any other wealth liabilities, you can only buy it when you can afford it. I would suggest you purchase your own home when your passive income would at least cover your mortgage payment.

Should I put any or more money in my retirement account?

It depends. If you can manage and invest your money at a better rate of return than what the retirement account is offering you, then don't. But if you are very risk averse, have read and understood the information in this book, and have decided not to invest by yourself at all, then do it. Do it knowing that your delayed gratification will not pay until you reach your retirement age, and which may not be enough even then. I personally would rather spend less, work hard now, invest my money now, and have the control of my retirement later. If you can accumulate enough financial wealth before retirement, you are financially savvy, and you know your retirement will be comfortable. And if your company pays you pension, be grateful and use it as a backup.

What's your take on a financial planner, accountant, or lawyer?

The good ones are your teammates; the bad ones are your bloodsucking vampires. The good ones save you from troubles, and they remind and advise you on important things. They empower you and want you to succeed. The bad ones hold back certain things purposely, making you totally dependable on them while charging you a fortune along the way. Shop around. Be comfortable with your adviser. Balance their intelligence and their personality. You are in for the long term with your advisers. It doesn't mean you can't change along the way. It's just better and more efficient to stick to one. Get to know one who is honest and empowers you with facts, not with fake praises.

What is your risk profile?

I always try to manage my risk. I don't tolerate being exposed to risk. I find out what my risks are, then I invest to reduce my risk. I protect myself, my family, my investment, and I diversify. I take control and minimize risk myself through the help of others. I don't give this role to anyone else. I invest in income-producing assets. I buy insurance to make sure that they are safeguarding the things I love. I diversify within asset classes as I progress, but I always focus on each asset at one time.

Do you believe in getting wealthy quick or slow?

Both have been proven to work. As long as the benefit outweighs the cost and it gives result, I don't see why the fuss. But in terms of preference, I'd prefer a quick financial freedom than the slow one. And I'm talking about five years quick compared to slow saving for forty years before becoming financially free. I know that there is no overnight success, but I want to explore the world when I'm young. Can you be wealthy next week? Possibly. There are money miracles. But they are rare and are never dependable for financial security or success. Money miracles do not make someone wealthy; they only give them more money, but without the money wisdom, they will lose it one way or another. A million dollar does not automatically make someone a millionaire.

You said that you know how to be rich, but how come you're not? I don't see your name on the rich list. Are you bluffing?

This is an interesting question. Now, the term *rich* is relative, but for the sake of this argument, I would say financially rich people are the top 10% of the population regardless of which country they live in. I've analyzed the financials of people with high net asset worth, and I've figured it out how they become financially wealthy. If they don't cook the book, then the numbers don't lie. You can see exactly where all the incomes are coming from.

I'm not bluffing because someone who truly knows how to be rich can say this statement upon all the information in this book: the information in this book is not enough if your aim is to be extremely rich. But I've said in the very beginning this is not a book on how to be rich but on how to be financially free. Those who are rich may say to me that I need to add certain things in this book if I want to teach others to be extremely rich. Again, that is not my purpose.

Am I holding things back? No. The information is out there, but it is very unlikely for me to write about how to be extremely rich. The title of this book is *Financial Freedom*, and being rich is out of the context. Again, my mission is to share with you wisdom on how to be financially free, and all the information contained in this book should be enough for you to know and understand it, but only you alone can determine the success of it by applying the information.

Know this: if you are rich or your ambition is to be rich, you will be tempted greatly, and not everyone can survive this temptation without a solid appreciation of God. The temptation to create profit out of apparently nothing, or exploit others' tragedies will be hard to resist. Greed may take over your rational thinking. And being greedy violate the mind-set of wealth. You may be doing a soft crime against humanity. Meaning, you don't get jailed if you indirectly harm or murder others for you to be rich. You may have more power than you deserve, and your real character will come out from this power. Unfortunately, those with massive power can only see one beneficiary of that power—themselves.

You may be tempted to try to overrule the law. All done while you are living in this delusional world that you think you will not suffer the consequences of your action. You will be oblivious in your dream bubble until it pops and it hits you really hard. Your life will be too focused on money. Don't kid yourself; having a lot of money demands your time and energy to manage it. You may lose yourself in the process. You may disrespect money and disrespect life as the consequences. You tend to corrupt anything and anyone who deals with you. If you don't like something, you'll try to make your money change it.

You may become arrogant. You may think money can give you anything. It becomes your God. You may judge others by how much money they have. Moreover, you may be crossing the moral and ethical lines. You may be exploiting others' tragedies, others' sufferings, to bring about massive gain to yourself. At the end of the day, you will indeed reap what you sow. Maybe not in this life, maybe not on yourself. But you will, and that's for certain. This is not a fear campaign. This is based on history and something you can validate yourself.

I'm not saying or judging or condemning that bad things will only happen to rich people. It happens to everyone, good and bad people, and I'm not claiming to know why it happens. I'm only pointing out to the fact that universal justice exists. Look, there is always room for people who have what it takes to be rich. It is not for everyone. Being rich puts you into a possible position of losing big, and not everyone can handle losing big.

So does that mean every exceptionally rich people are bad people? I don't know. Who am I to know the content of someone's heart? Rich people are still people. I don't see how their money represents them. Stop monetizing everything. Look at the person as a person, not how much they physically have.

Think that if they lose all their money, would you still be friends with them? Position and wealth often act as illusions of the real person. A person's worth cannot be determined by how much money one has. I would look at their actions for their characters. If I do their tax return and it shows that they've earned millions but they donated zero, well, that says a lot about them. The point is, success is determined by how much you give, not by how much you have. Taking is technical; everyone is able and willing to make a profit. Giving is something else. Not everyone is able and willing to do it. Therefore, it is scarcer. And anything scarce is more valuable than the plenty. Obviously, there are people who are rich while sticking to their morality compass. But again, the world's morality is relative. Some people think it's okay to be in the gray zone; some stay strictly on the black-and-white zone.

Just be content with what you have. It's always easier to look up than to look down. Think of all those people who are still trading time for money, who are living in fear for their lives every single day, who experience excruciating physical, emotional, and spiritual pains every day. You're in so much better position, so much so that if you still want more, only selfishness and greediness can drive you. And selfishness and greediness work like drugs.

The first time you satisfy your greed, it gives you a rush. The next time, it will give you less, but you're expecting more. This cycle goes on to the point of numbing you. What you take doesn't make you happy anymore. It is then when you switch to the real drugs. And the real drugs kill you. Think of giving instead. You may not get a rush the first time you share your wealth, but if your motive is right, even a small gift can bring a smile to your soul. And over time if you genuinely keep sharing things, your self-worth, your self-appreciation will increase. It is most commonly called joy. Living a joyful life on a constant basis. Don't we all want that?

So let us be humble and think, wouldn't it be enough and unbelievably amazing to have a passive income covering all your expenses so you're free to use your time? It forces you to control yourself. Receiving a relatively smaller but regular income is healthier for you than receiving one massive lump sum.

There is so much more in life, and focusing on being rich means you're risking cutting your life short. You'll be sacrificing too much to get too little. You'll focus solely on money and less on wealth. You will think that you are not dependent on anything, not even on God Himself. You will have less faith and be the first who stumbles upon difficulties. You'll become weak because you are not rooted to the source of wealth. If you look at the big picture, you can really honestly think that we cannot boast on anything.

And being *rich* doesn't necessarily mean being free. Some work hard for almost 24-7, and some die young from stress. There are numerous cases where someone works so hard for money thinking they still have the time and energy to double or even triple their money only to be told by the doctor that they have about three months to sort out their affairs. Tragic. Such a beautiful life wasted on chasing paper money. Too bad people don't realize that you can't do anything when you're dead. Once you're dead, that's it. You cannot have and enjoy sex, you cannot drink and enjoy beer, and you cannot feel alive. You cannot do things that pleases you in life.

Every second you waste is gone. But that doesn't mean you have to rush to get everything you want in life. You want to enjoy everything this life can offer. That's why everyone is clinging to life. Just remember that wealth is the product of the mind and therefore, cannot be satisfied with a physical product. Beware of the old sneaky offer "Why only one if you can have two?" And lastly, think about this, how many cents will the richest person bring along to the other side when he or she dies? Not even half a cent. Nothing in their physical possessions will be carried over. Only their spiritual possessions. We were born out of spirit with no physical possession, and we will return with no physical posession into the spirit world. Despite all these, I still have faith in the good people of society who may want to be rich because they have a genuinely noble agenda. To those, I can only say, big things can only come when you're faithful with little things.

In closing, love yourself and others. When you love yourself you will not be selfish and greedy for you'll know that greed is not good for anyone. Because when you take and never give, your life will turn rancid just like piling up on food and never using it. And when you suffer from your greed, everyone around you will too. Just remember that there will be times when it matters not what you have, but what you've given away freely. There will be times when money doesn't mean anything at all. At that time, love will be the only currency. And you will either be short-changed, or in abundance. To end a life in regret, hate, and pain, or to be able to honestly say to yourself that "I lived a good life, I lived a life of love. I had no regret." And people would remember your love. You would live and die in happiness.

Epilogue

Ask yourself why don't you try? Why not you? Why not now? Why postpone a better future? Why not use the gift of life, now when it is still available?

At the end of the day, we will all leave a legacy, good or bad. People will either cry or rejoice at our departure from this world. So think about our future obituary. Can we satisfactorily answer these two questions on our deathbed: Did I live? And did I love? You will be a very happy and peaceful person leaving the earth knowing that you are significant, that you matter. Anyone who lives his or her life well means he or she loves well, and anyone who loves is loved. You will have the priceless satisfaction that you've used the gift of life gratefully, and your family, friends, and the world at large have been blessed abundantly by your presence in this world.

I hope that you now focus on living your life
and less on seeking money.

I hope that you now focus on giving
and less on taking.

I hope that you now focus on being happy
and less on pursuing happiness.

I hope that you now realize that life is never about giving up
but about ever discovering ourselves.

When you fall down, remember that this too shall pass.
Tears can indeed be the beginning of a better future.

When you rise up, be humble always.
No one has achieved anything alone.

Celebrate every day because your days are very precious,
and therefore, there is no such thing as a bad day.

Celebrate life every day because we are enjoying something
we didn't help to create.

Celebrate love every day because every day
is your birthday and Christmas day and Valentine's day.

Love is when you give, not expecting anything in return, yet receive.
We are the source of love. Out of love we were born,
and to love we shall return and find comforting peace.

May love complete you and give you real and lasting happiness.

May love give that special someone who catches your fall and lifts you up
to be the best you can be because to appreciate each other's strengths
and to bear each other's weaknesses is what they call the art of love.

And finally, act justly, love mercy, and walk humbly with your God.

Thank you and God bless.

WWW.ONTHEGOSERIES.COM

We created this series because honest, complete, and practical information is needed on many other important topics in life. So it is now your turn to share. We know that the experts are not the only ones who have the solutions to our problems. We, the everyday people who go through things personally, usually have them too. Therefore we invite you to share your personal success stories in any of the upcoming titles to help others overcome their problems. If your unique story, idea, or suggestion is included in any of our series, you will receive a free book on the titles you help create. The upcoming titles include:

> *Weight Loss, Leadership, Diabetes Type II, Emotional Intelligence, Insomnia, Asthma, Healthy Cooking, Communication Skills, Allergies, Spirituality, Anxiety & Depression, and many more.*

We are also currently building programs to help you apply the information on any of our books. We are confident that the information provided on each topic is enough, but we are also here for you if you need a helping hand to implement it in your life.

And finally, we always love to hear from you, our dearest reader and we would like to extend our warm welcome for your feedback and participation. Visit us on **www.onthegoseries.com** and contact us at **info@onthegoseries.com**. We can't promise to reply to everyone. But we promise to try.

WWW.FACEBOOK.COM/ SOCIALJUSTICEAUSTRALIA

Social Justice Australia is a national project to bring about equality, fairness, and solidarity for all Australians.

Our first project is to raise awareness by creating a documentary that will look at the reality of Australia's social injustice in form of poverty, discrimination, unfair policies, greed, and the shrinking middle class in Australia, but more importantly to show how we, the people, are so capable to make long-lasting and positive changes now. It will also uniquely provides instant assistance to the audience via its interactive generic financial lesson at the end of the program, seeking to benefit the most important thing for their welfare, their minds.

But the documentary is a mere launching pad for a national movement, aiming to bring about real, positive, and measurable change. It's about mateship and fair go, about taking care of each other's back, about the Australia all Australians deserve. The question now is whether we as Australians know about this, and whether they are willing to commit and solve this problem once and for all.

Our first goal is to get 100,000 followers on our Facebook page. Show to this nation that we care about each other. We are not looking for financial donation, only your support, solidarity, and love for others.